LinkedIn® in One Hour
FOR LAWYERS

DENNIS KENNEDY AND ALLISON C. SHIELDS

ABA LawPracticeManagementSection
MARKETING • MANAGEMENT • TECHNOLOGY • FINANCE

LinkedIn® is a registered trademark of the LinkedIn® Corporation.

Cover design by RIPE Creative, Inc.

Nothing contained in this book is to be considered as the rendering of legal advice for specific cases, and readers are responsible for obtaining such advice from their own legal counsel. This book and any forms and agreements herein are intended for educational and informational purposes only.

The products and services mentioned in this publication are under or may be under trademark or service mark protection. Product and service names and terms are used throughout only in an editorial fashion, to the benefit of the product manufacturer or service provider, with no intention of infringement. Use of a product or service name or term in this publication should not be regarded as affecting the validity of any trademark or service mark.

The Law Practice Management Section, American Bar Association, offers an educational program for lawyers in practice. Books and other materials are published in furtherance of that program. Authors and editors of publications may express their own legal interpretations and opinions, which are not necessarily those of either the American Bar Association or the Law Practice Management Section unless adopted pursuant to the bylaws of the Association. The opinions expressed do not reflect in any way a position of the Section or the American Bar Association.

Printed in the United States of America

ISBN 978-1-61438-348-2

15 14 13 12   5 4 3 2

Library of Congress Cataloging-in-Publication Data

Kennedy, Dennis M., 1958–
   LinkedIn in one hour for lawyers / Dennis Kennedy and Allison Shields.
      p. cm.
   Includes index.
   ISBN 978-1-61438-348-2
   1. Internet in legal services—United States. 2. Online social networks—Law and legislation—United States. 3. Social media—Law and legislation—United States. 4. Law offices—United States—Computer network resources. I. Shields, Allison (Allison C.), 1969– II. Title.
   KF320.A9K46   2012
   340.0285'53—dc23
                                                                                    2012004903

Discounts are available for books ordered in bulk. Special consideration is given to state bars, CLE programs, and other bar-related organizations. Inquire at Book Publishing, American Bar Association, 321 N. Clark Street, Chicago, Illinois 60654.

www.ShopABA.org

Table of Contents

About the Authors v

Acknowledgments vii

Introduction: *What Is LinkedIn, Why So Many Lawyers Use It,
and Why You Should Too* 1

THE LESSONS

LESSON ONE: *Setting Up an Account: Choosing Between
Basic and Premium Account Options* 7

LESSON TWO: *Completing Your Basic Profile* 11

LESSON THREE: *Creating a Robust, Dynamic Profile* 19

LESSON FOUR: *Getting Started with Connections* 25

LESSON FIVE: *Making Even More Connections* 35

LESSON SIX: *Using LinkedIn Search* 43

LESSON SEVEN: *Participating on LinkedIn Using Updates
and Groups* 51

LESSON EIGHT: *Benefiting from LinkedIn Answers and
Recommendations* 59

LESSON NINE: *Monitoring Your Network* 67

LESSON TEN: *Optimizing Your Settings* 75

CONCLUSION: *Developing a Simple LinkedIn Strategy and
Three Action Steps* 81

ADVANCED TOPICS

Ethical Considerations 85

Using LinkedIn in the Hiring Process 95

LinkedIn Apps 99

Company Pages 103

Advanced Search Techniques 107

Sixty LinkedIn Tips 115

Resources 121

Index 125

About the Authors

Dennis Kennedy is an information technology lawyer, as well as a widely published author and frequent speaker on legal technology and Internet topics. He writes the technology column for the *ABA Journal,* co-authored with Tom Mighell the book, *The Lawyer's Guide to Collaboration Tools: Smart Ways to Work Together*, and co-hosts the popular legal technology podcast, "The Kennedy-Mighell Report," on the Legal Talk Network. His blog, **http://denniskennedy.com/blog/**, is a highly regarded resource on technology law and legal technology topics.

Allison C. Shields is the author of the Legal Ease Blog (**www.legaleaseconsulting.com**) and president of Legal Ease Consulting, Inc., where she coaches lawyers on practice management and business development issues, including social media and Internet marketing. She is a former practicing lawyer, law firm manager, and administrative partner. A nationally recognized speaker, Ms. Shields presents workshops and programs in both private and public settings. She is also the author of numerous articles on practice management and business development/marketing issues. Ms. Shields' Web site, Lawyer Meltdown (**www.LawyerMeltdown.com**), provides resources and information for lawyers about managing and building their practices.

Acknowledgments

To Tim Johnson, for suggesting the book idea, convincing us to take on the project, managing the process and giving us great suggestions after reading the first draft; to the great team on the American Bar Association's Law Practice Management Section publishing staff, for turning our draft into the finished book you are reading; to the Law Practice Management Section Book Publishing Board, for letting us write on this important topic; to Michelle Golden, for participating in the great Webinar that prompted this book; to Carole Levitt, for her helpful, detailed comments on the first draft of this book; to Grace Kennedy, for proofreading and other editing assistance; and to our families, for their patience, understanding, and support during the book writing process and all of the rest of the time as well.

Introduction

What Is LinkedIn,
Why So Many Lawyers Use It,
and Why You Should Too

Lawyers live and move in a world of interlocking, evolving networks of people. Lawyers connect on a daily basis with formal and informal networks of colleagues, clients, opposing counsel, service providers, experts, and others who are essential to the successful practice of law. Lawyers use these connections to get referrals and recommendations, obtain information, move projects and cases forward, and assist their clients.

Founded in 2003, LinkedIn passed the 100 million registered users mark in 2011, making it the premier business social networking tool today. In contrast to other social media tools, LinkedIn emphasizes professional networking.

Even the lawyers most wary of "social media" will consider using LinkedIn. The very terms "friending" on Facebook and "tweeting" on Twitter make many lawyers reluctant to try other social media tools. On the other hand, LinkedIn's universe of Profiles and Connections and its emphasis on professional relationships just make sense to most lawyers.

A 2011 report, *Global Social Media Check Up: A Global Audit of Law Firm Engagement in Social Media Methods* from LexisNexis' Martindale Hubbell division (see Resources), indicates that LinkedIn has 770,000 members in the legal field, making the legal sector the fifth largest on LinkedIn.

The report confirms other surveys and our own informal polling when we speak about social media for lawyers that a large percentage of lawyers are registered LinkedIn users. The emphasis is on "registered" users. Lawyers often tell us that they barely use LinkedIn and would like to learn to use LinkedIn better or more effectively than they do now. What they mean is that they do not understand the basic features.

Before you dive into this book, we suggest you take a few minutes to think about how many people you talk to and work with in the average day or week. It might surprise you. If you map out on paper the people you know and the relationships between you and the people in some of the categories we mentioned (e.g., colleagues, clients, providers), you will quickly see how rich and complex your networks can be, even if you are a solo practitioner.

If you then consider the ways in which your networks allow you to tap into the similar networks of your connections for recommendations and referrals, you will see the value of "who you know" and "who they know" in your professional practice. Lawyers who do well for themselves, their clients, and those they work with often have long-standing, well-nurtured, and thriving networks.

LinkedIn is a tool to help you make your networks more visible and usable than they are when they are only in your head. It lets you map your networks, organize them, grow and nurture them, and efficiently use them both for your own benefit and the benefit of your connections. It does so in a simple, easy-to-understand way that works very well for lawyers with results you can see and measure.

There are three essential parts of your LinkedIn presence that you must understand well: Profiles, Connections, and Participation. If you get these pieces right, you will "get" LinkedIn and should find it a valuable use of your time.

- **Profiles** establish your presence and professional identity on LinkedIn. Your Profile is an online, living professional biography or resume that lets others know, in detail, who you are. Your Profile is your "face" on LinkedIn.

- **Connections** are the people in your networks. LinkedIn lets you identify people in your existing networks, find new people to meet, and invite them all to connect to you. By accepting invitations to connect, people show that they are connected professionally.
- **Participation** is the cultivating and tending of your Connections in your network. It is the way you engage with members of your network. Lawyers who have joined LinkedIn but say they have found no value often have neglected this crucial aspect. Properly understood, social media is participatory media. You must put effort into your online networking in similar ways to what you do in your real-world networks.

This book is organized into two major sections: Lessons and Advanced Topics. In the Lessons section, we cover key subjects to get you quickly up to speed on LinkedIn, whether you are a beginner or a long-time user. The Lessons are the core of the book. In the Advanced Topics section, we cover some important issues (such as legal ethics), advanced features, and resources so that you can dive deeper into LinkedIn and use it more effectively. The idea is that you can read the entire book in about one hour, but you can also focus on a specific topic as you work with LinkedIn. Think of the book as a friendly companion to keep beside you as you use LinkedIn.

Our Agenda
- **Lesson 1: Setting Up an Account: Choosing Between Basic and Premium Account Options.** We cover the basics of opening or revitalizing your account and compare the basic and premium LinkedIn account options.
- **Lesson 2: Completing Your Basic Profile.** Profiles are one of the three essential LinkedIn building blocks. We show you how to get started by completing a basic Profile.

- **Lesson 3: Creating a Robust, Dynamic Profile.** Unlike a standard resume or biography in a brochure, your Profile can be active and dynamic. We discuss ways to take advantage of advanced Profile features to put your Profile to work for you.

- **Lesson 4: Getting Started with Connections.** The second essential LinkedIn building block is Connections—the people in your network. We provide three powerful techniques to help you ramp up your network quickly and keep it growing.

- **Lesson 5: Making Even More Connections.** There is no excuse for having only a handful of LinkedIn Connections from your real-world networks. We show you five more techniques to add Connections to your network.

- **Lesson 6: Using LinkedIn Search.** LinkedIn's search tools are impressive. We introduce to the power of LinkedIn searching and filtering.

- **Lesson 7: Participating on LinkedIn Using Updates and Groups.** Participation is the third essential building block of LinkedIn. We cover Updates and Groups, the two participation tools you will want to use to obtain information about your Connections or find new people with whom to connect.

- **Lesson 8: Benefiting from LinkedIn Answers and Recommendations.** Lawyers have found other LinkedIn participation tools to be beneficial. We discuss two more participation tools: Answers and Recommendations.

- **Lesson 9: Monitoring Your Network.** You must cultivate and tend to your Connections and network. We introduce you to some of LinkedIn's great monitoring tools: the Homepage, e-mail notifications, and the mobile app.

- **Lesson 10: Optimizing Your Settings.** Privacy in social media can be a minefield for lawyers. We emphasize the importance of getting your privacy and account settings right and show you how to adjust and manage your settings.

■ **Conclusion: Developing a Simple LinkedIn Strategy and Three Action Steps.** We wrap up our Lessons with some help on determining your LinkedIn strategies and provide three action steps to enhance LinkedIn's value to you.

■ **Advanced Topics.** In this section, we provide a quick overview of advanced topics, issues especially of interest to lawyers, and tips to improve your use of LinkedIn, including:
  ► Ethical considerations
  ► LinkedIn in the hiring process
  ► LinkedIn's useful apps
  ► Company and firm features
  ► Advanced search techniques
  ► Sixty tips
  ► Helpful resources

There is no question that LinkedIn is currently, and likely will remain, the number one social media tool for lawyers. LinkedIn's emphasis on professional networking and its alignment with the professional approach lawyers prefer make it well suited to lawyers' needs. LinkedIn itself recognizes the importance of the tool for lawyers. On the LinkedIn Support page, **http://learn.linkedin.com/attorneys/,** you will find a user guide specifically for lawyers.

It is not just "who you know" literally that makes the biggest difference in the success of your practice, but how you create, nurture, and maintain a community of those "who you know." That is what LinkedIn offers and what this book will help you use it for.

Let us get started with Lesson 1.

Setting Up an Account
Choosing Between Basic and Premium Account Options

Even though LinkedIn debuted in 2003, it is not too late to get started. In fact, you can start right now and, by the time you finish this book, be among the best users of LinkedIn among lawyers. We commonly hear lawyers tell us that they have a LinkedIn account but have never really done anything with it. Our goal is to change that.

LinkedIn is an online service, not a software program. In fact, LinkedIn is a good example of "cloud computing." There is no software to install, and you do not have to have a certain type of computer—just a computer connected to the Internet. You can use LinkedIn anytime and anywhere you have Internet access, whether at home, work, or with a mobile device.

In this first Lesson, we will help you create or reactivate your LinkedIn account. The process is simple and familiar for anyone who has ever set up any online account. We end the Lesson by helping you decide whether a basic LinkedIn account will work for you or whether you will want a premium account.

Confirming or Setting Up Your Account

Do you have a working LinkedIn account? Readers of this book will fall into three categories:

1) If you already have a LinkedIn account, know your password, and can log into your account, skip directly to the section on basic and premium accounts below.

2) If you already have a LinkedIn account, but no longer know your password and cannot log into your account, you must reset your password and confirm that you can log into your account. Go to the LinkedIn Web site and attempt to log into your account using the e-mail address you used when you set up the account and what you think your password is. If this fails, attempt to have the password reset by clicking on the "Forgot Password?" link. LinkedIn will send you an e-mail with a new temporary password. Log in using the link in the e-mail and change to a new password that you will now remember or store securely. Once you can log into your account, skip to the section on basic and premium accounts below.

   It is possible that you will find that you started your LinkedIn account using an e-mail address you can no longer access (e.g., an e-mail address from a former law firm). In that case, the password reset option will not be available, and you must set up a new LinkedIn account using another e-mail address following the steps below. A personal Gmail or other Webmail address that you expect to keep for a long time might be a good choice.

3) If you do not have a LinkedIn account, you must register a new account. Setting up a new account is similar to setting up an account with any other Web service. Go to the LinkedIn Web site at **http://www.linkedin.com**. Complete the form called "Join LinkedIn Today" on the right and click on "Join Now" (see Figure 1.1).

   When you receive the confirming e-mail from LinkedIn (probably in a matter of seconds), click on the link in the e-mail and log into your new LinkedIn account.

Figure 1.1: Start Page

Choosing the Basic or Premium Account

For most lawyers, the basic (and free!) LinkedIn account will work well. Be aware, however, that LinkedIn offers a variety of premium accounts that range in cost from $19.95 to $99.95 per month. Premium account owners enjoy enhanced features like more powerful search, analytics, and communications tools and increased access to other users. To learn more, click on the "Account Type" link at the top of any page once you have logged in (see Figure 1.2).

Figure 1.2: Account Type Link

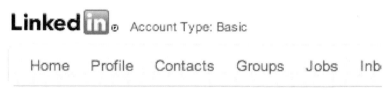

You will be taken to a page that describes the Premium account options and the additional features you will receive for the additional costs (see Figure 1.3).

Figure 1.3: Premium Account Features

You must evaluate the additional features and whether they make sense for you. A premium account might make sense for legal marketing professionals or during a job search, but the basic free account will be sufficient for most readers of this book. If you change your mind and want to upgrade later, it is easy to do so. LinkedIn gives you several ways to find your way to the upgrade options, included under the "More" tab at the top of each page.

We cover the important topic of account settings, including privacy, in Lesson 10.

Let us now move to Lesson 2, where we help you establish your identity with one of the three essential LinkedIn building blocks: your Profile.

Completing Your Basic Profile

Your firm or personal Web site is your "home base" online, and your Profile is your "home base" on LinkedIn. Your Profile is where people go to find out information about you, and it is where much of your LinkedIn content resides. You can also think of your Profile as an online "living" resume or biography.

Building Your Initial Profile

When you set up your account, LinkedIn will automatically get you started on your professional Profile. The first few screens you encounter after you set up your account will ask questions about your current employment, which is automatically transferred to your Profile. However, the initial information you enter when you set up your LinkedIn account is just the first step in creating a complete LinkedIn Profile. In this Lesson, we will take you through the rest of the steps to compile your Profile.

To fully complete your Profile, you must go to the "Edit Profile" button located under the Profile tab on the main navigation bar (see Figure 2.1).

Figure 2.1: Edit Profile

You can input Profile information by hand, but LinkedIn also offers a great way to automate the process. If you have a resume readily available, LinkedIn allows you to upload it, which makes building your Profile a bit faster. Simply click on the "Import your resume" button, find the document on your computer, and follow the directions to upload it. LinkedIn will import the information from your resume and populate the appropriate fields on your Profile. The fields are fully editable so that you can pick and choose which information you want to include.

Once uploaded, LinkedIn will request that you review the information before it is published to your LinkedIn Profile. Even if the information appears correct, we recommend that you click on "Edit" so that you can revise or update as necessary for the LinkedIn audience. Click on "Save Changes," and the information will be published to your LinkedIn Profile.

Editing Your Profile

To edit your Profile once you have registered for your account and input the initial Profile information (or uploaded your resume), click on "Edit Profile" and then look for the small "Edit" buttons (see Figure 2.2).

Figure 2.2: Edit Buttons

Profile Photo

Your photograph is an important part of your LinkedIn Profile. Professional photographs are preferable, but do not wait until you have time to get around to having a professional photograph taken. It is perfectly acceptable to use a high-quality digital photograph from your own digital camera or a cropped family or personal photograph of your face—so long as it looks professional and presents you well. Why is your photograph important?

- People may recognize your face before they remember your name
- Many people use LinkedIn to prepare for a meeting; having a photograph on LinkedIn makes you easier to recognize
- People do business with people they know, like, and trust; posting a photograph helps your audience feel that they "know" you

Click on the "Add Photo" button and upload the photograph from your computer, or to upload a new photograph in place of your old one, click on "Edit Photo" under your picture.

Profile Link

Make it easier to find, advertise, and share your LinkedIn Profile. Edit the "public Profile link" generated when you create your Profile. It looks something like this: **http://www.linkedin.com/pub/john-smith/26/4a1/114.**

Get rid of the random numbers and letters to customize the link to include just your name, a keyword or two, or your name and firm name by clicking on "Edit" next to your public Profile link (see Figure 2.2, at the bottom of the image).

Other Links

LinkedIn allows three links in the Profile. You can link to your Web site, blog, firm bio, etc. Use all three opportunities, but do not use LinkedIn's default settings for the link titles (e.g., "Company Website").

Customize the link titles by clicking "Edit" next to them on the Edit Profile screen. Choose "other" in the first box and create your own name for the link. Use keywords or the actual name of your firm or site. If you have only one law firm Web site, use one to link to your firm Web site's home page and one to link to your individual biography on the firm site. Use the third to link to another profile of you on the Internet, your blog, or the firm page for your practice group.

Professional Headline

Your professional headline is a one-line description that often accompanies your name when you interact on LinkedIn. The professional headline field defaults to your current title. You can change this to make it much more descriptive and useful by clicking "Edit" next to your name.

Instead of just your title or insider firm descriptions ("associate" or "partner"), use all of the 120 characters allotted in the Professional Headline field and provide information helpful to someone outside your firm. Describe your practice area, your clients, or your services and make sure you use "lawyer" or "attorney" in your description for those all-important search results.

Summary

Next is the "Summary" field, which consists of two separate sections. "Professional Experience and Goals" allows 2,000 characters (approximately 330 words) of description. This field appears at the top of the Profile. Because your summary often is read more than the description under your current position, do not overlook it. Describe what you do. Make it interesting. Consider it a chance to give your "elevator pitch."

"Specialties" is a shorter section (256 total characters), usually written with keywords rather than in narrative format (think one- to three-word bullet points rather than longer descriptive sentences). If you are concerned about ethical prohibitions against lawyers identifying themselves as "specialists" in a particular field, include a disclaimer indicating that rather than specialties, you have listed your practice areas instead. (We discuss the "specialties" issue further in the ethics discussion in the Advanced Topics section.)

Experience/Positions

Positions display in your Profile under "Experience" in reverse chronological order. List all of your relevant past and present experience and positions, including the name of the company or firm for which you worked, the dates you worked there, your title, and a description of what you did. Use keywords that are important to and recognizable by your target audience. Include important experience or skills that help to differentiate you from other lawyers in your field. You have 1,000 characters to describe each position. Be complete in adding all of your previous positions. We will discuss in Lesson 4 how LinkedIn uses this information to help you connect to current and former colleagues.

You may list bar association or other community positions (such as board service, etc.) here, too. Listing these activities helps others find you when they search for the organization name and makes it easier to invite others associated with that organization to connect.

Be aware that LinkedIn will list your positions in reverse chronological order and this cannot be changed. This may result in bar or other volunteer positions appearing ahead of your law practice. Alternatively, you may choose to list these positions under "Groups and Associations" in the "Additional Information" section or in the optional "Organizations" section.

Education

School alumni can be valuable contacts, as we discuss in Lesson 4. Include your educational information, both for your law school and for any undergraduate or other post-secondary education.

Making Your Profile Complete

As you build your LinkedIn Profile, you will see a "completeness bar" on the right side of the screen that measures how complete your Profile is (see Figure 2.3). Your goal is a Profile that is considered "100% complete."

Figure 2.3: Completeness Bar

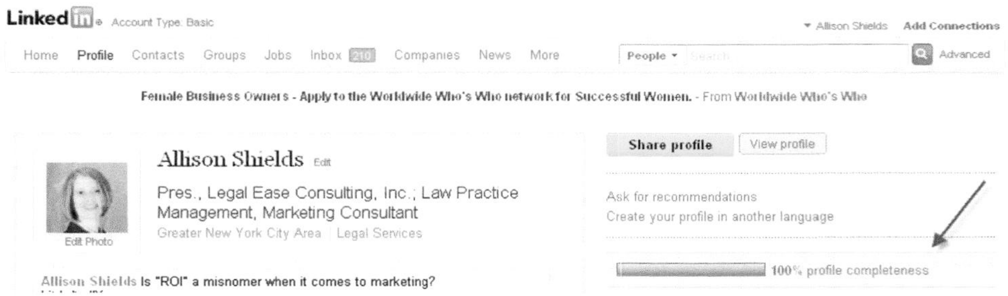

LinkedIn considers your Profile "100% complete" when it contains:

- Your current position
- Two past positions
- Your education
- Your Profile summary
- Your Profile photo
- Your specialties (remember to consider the ethical issues discussed in the Advanced Topics section of this book)
- At least three recommendations (we will cover Recommendations in Lesson 8 and ethical considerations relating to Recommendations in the Advanced Topics section of this book)

We recommend that you spend some time completing your Profile, but it does not need to be done in one sitting. If you commit to spending only fifteen minutes or so per day to completing the basic sections of your Profile mentioned in this Lesson, you will have a completed Profile in a few days without feeling overwhelmed. If you begin by importing your current resume, the process can be completed quickly.

Even when your Profile is considered "100% complete," there are additional steps you can take to make it more robust and more searchable. To learn how to do that, let us move to Lesson 3.

Creating a Robust, Dynamic Profile

Why Improve Your Profile?

Now that your basic Profile has been completed and you are more familiar with the LinkedIn interface, let us talk about making your Profile really stand out. There are several good reasons to have as complete a Profile as possible on LinkedIn.

LinkedIn as a Marketing Tool

First and foremost, your LinkedIn Profile is a marketing document. It is your online ambassador. If potential clients or referral sources find you on LinkedIn, you want them to have as much information about you at their fingertips as possible, and you want it to present you in the best light possible. The more comprehensive your Profile, the more reasons people have to connect or engage with you.

Improve Your Search Engine Visibility

Second, a Profile containing details about you and your practice areas will improve your online visibility. When someone has been referred to you or already knows your name, they are likely to vet you online by conducting a Google search. Your LinkedIn Profile may be the first result they see in a long list of search results.

Even if the individual searching does not already have your name, the more information you have available in your LinkedIn Profile, the better your chances of showing up in the search engines for relevant terms because LinkedIn is so large and so optimized for search. Content is still king. Provide content on your LinkedIn Profile with relevant keywords that your potential clients and referral sources might use to search for a lawyer or for information in your practice area or area of expertise.

Be More Visible within LinkedIn

Third, the more complete your Profile, the more likely your Profile will be found for searches *within* LinkedIn. LinkedIn indicates that users with complete Profiles might be forty times more likely to receive opportunities through LinkedIn than those with incomplete Profiles. As you will see in Lesson 6, LinkedIn has robust search capabilities, but you cannot be found if your information is not there.

The LinkedIn search algorithm uses your Profile to determine your relevance to others searching on the site for Companies, Connections, or individuals with particular skills or experience. Even if you *are* found, it is much more likely that someone will want to connect or engage with you if your Profile is complete. Missing information can be frustrating to other LinkedIn users. Completeness demonstrates transparency and the care you take in presenting yourself to others.

Manage Your Reputation and Your Personal Brand

Fourth, a completed Profile helps you manage your reputation online. Whether you work for yourself or are part of a firm, you have a personal brand. Perhaps you do not have your own Web site or blog, or you work for a firm that does not have a satisfactory Web presence or content online. You can still build your personal brand through LinkedIn and provide others (including strategic alliances, potential referral sources, and potential employers) with a comprehensive view of your professional skills and capabilities. You cannot always control what others might say about you, but you can provide high-quality content that demonstrates your expertise. Why squander the opportunity?

Find the Right Job

Fifth, if you are a lawyer in search of a job, your LinkedIn Profile may be just as important as—if not more important than—your resume. We discuss the use of LinkedIn in the hiring process in more detail in the Advanced Topics section of this book.

How to Improve Your Profile

To continually improve your Profile over time, click on the yellow "Improve your Profile" button to the right of the Edit Profile screen, and LinkedIn will walk you step by step through some suggestions for building a more robust Profile. LinkedIn also shows you how much these improvements will increase your "completeness" percentage (see Figure 3.1).

Figure 3.1: Improve Your Profile

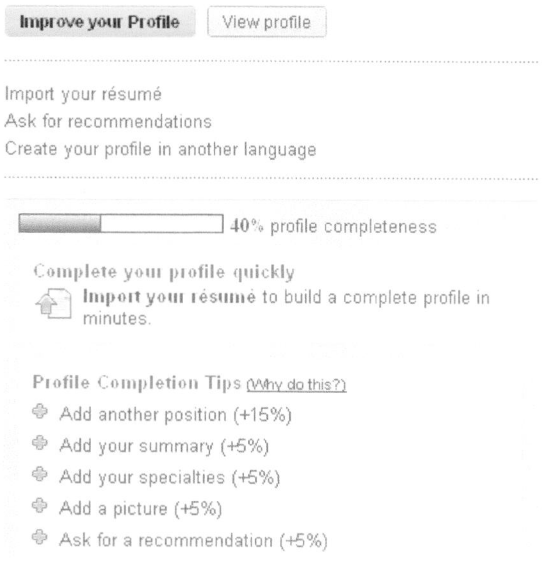

Improve your Profile   View profile

Import your résumé
Ask for recommendations
Create your profile in another language

[▬▬▬▬▬▬] 40% profile completeness

Complete your profile quickly
  Import your résumé to build a complete profile in minutes.

Profile Completion Tips (Why do this?)
✦ Add another position (+15%)
✦ Add your summary (+5%)
✦ Add your specialties (+5%)
✦ Add a picture (+5%)
✦ Ask for a recommendation (+5%)

You can also improve your Profile by clicking on the "Add Sections" button that appears just below your basic Profile information on the Edit Profile screen (see Figure 3.2). This will bring you to a screen with a list of sections that you can add to your LinkedIn Profile.

Figure 3.2: Edit Profile Screen—Add Sections

Two of the most useful sections for lawyers are Publications and Skills.

Publications

Published books and articles, whether in print or online, add to your credibility and help establish your expertise by demonstrating what you know. LinkedIn allows you to list the title, publication, date, a brief description, and a link to the content if it is online.

Skills

Thinking about "skills" may be a bit foreign for lawyers, but as you will see in Lesson 6, LinkedIn returns search results directly linked to the Skills listed in your Profile; therefore, it is important to add something to this section for the best search results possible.

Skills can include not only your practice areas, but also the skills you use within those practice areas, such as negotiating contracts or trial advocacy. Completing this section is an opportunity to highlight specific skills that potential clients (or potential employers) might be seeking. For example, if you do continuing legal education or other public speaking, add speaking skills to help those looking for potential speakers find you.

Additional sections to enhance to your Profile include:

- Certifications (especially good for lawyers who are certified specialists in a specific area of the law)
- Languages (allowing you to showcase your fluency in other languages and target clients who may speak other languages)
- Organizations (organizations you belong to or are affiliated with, but not employed by)
- Projects
- Applications (we will discuss Applications in the Advanced Topics section of this book)

Tips for Making Your Profile Stand Out

- Use bullet points, not long paragraphs
- Compose your entries in a word processing program, then cut and paste into LinkedIn
- Utilize keywords in your content
- Speak your clients' language—use the terms that they use to describe their problem or situation
- Be interesting—make your experience come alive
- Use stories to illustrate what you do for clients
- Rearrange your Profile to put the most relevant information in a prominent position; roll your mouse over the section title and then drag and drop using the "handles" to rearrange your Profile sections

With a complete Profile in place, now it is time to move on to Lesson 4 and the beginning of the second essential building block of LinkedIn: Connections.

Getting Started with Connections

The second essential building block of LinkedIn is Connections. LinkedIn offers some great Connection tools to map out and populate your network. By building a solid LinkedIn network with good Connections, you will create a foundation that will help you get the most value out of LinkedIn.

Connecting Principles

The easiest way to understand LinkedIn's approach to Connections is to think in terms of "six degrees of separation." The idea, often associated with the actor Kevin Bacon, is that if we map our contacts to our contacts' contacts, to our contacts' contacts' contacts, and so on, we will be able to get from any person on the planet to any other person on the planet within six steps. LinkedIn adopts this notion of degrees of separation and will map the steps of relationship from you to anyone else. As we will discuss later in the book, you are able to do more with a first-degree relation than with a second- or third-degree relation, just as in real life.

LinkedIn also uses a "symmetrical" approach to social networking. Social media tools like Twitter (where you "follow" people) or Google+ (where you add people to Circles) use an "asymmetrical" approach— I can follow you even if you do not follow me back. In LinkedIn (and Facebook), I can add you as a Connection of mine only if you affirmatively accept my invitation to become a Connection, and vice versa. The result is that we have a confirmation that there is some kind of mutually agreed relationship between LinkedIn Connections.

Before jumping in to add Connections, decide on a guiding principle or two about how you want to add Connections and grow your network (quality vs. quantity, local vs. national, real world vs. Internet, internal vs. external, etc.). Checking the number of contacts you have in Outlook or in another address book will be a good place to start in terms of thinking about the approach you want to take on LinkedIn.

Getting a Running Start

LinkedIn now has great tools for adding Connections. If your experience with LinkedIn dates several years back, you will be pleasantly surprised at how much easier it has become to add people. In the early days, adding someone as a Connection often involved several e-mails where you needed to explain to the people you invited what LinkedIn was and then wait for them to set up their own accounts. Put those bad memories out of your mind.

In this Lesson, we will show you three powerful ways to add contacts to your LinkedIn network. You can use one, two, or all three of these methods based on what seems to work best for you. Many lawyers begin with LinkedIn but never add more than a handful of Connections. If you fall into that category or are just starting out, you can get off to a running start. Even if you already have a substantial list of Connections, we recommend that you supplement your current Connections list with these three techniques.

Simply enough, you will be working primarily under the "Contacts" menu and the "Add Connections" submenu under that for most of these methods (see Figure 4.1). The "Add Connections" option is also available in the top right hand corner from any page.

Figure 4.1: Add Connections

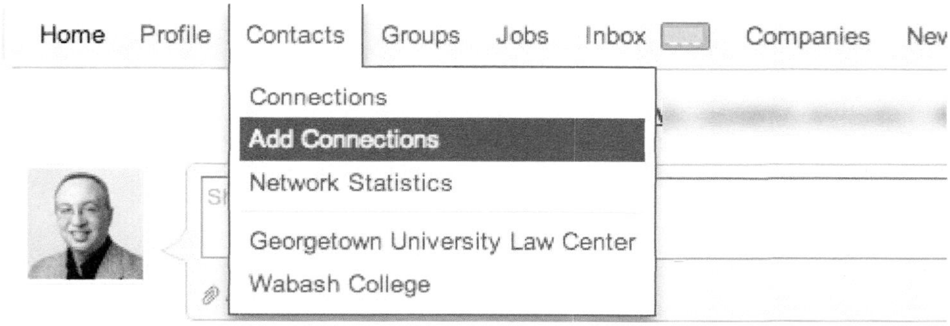

Method 1: Mining Your Contacts— The Automated Approach

Importing existing contacts is a great way to get started with LinkedIn Connections. LinkedIn makes it very easy to coordinate your LinkedIn Connections with your current contacts in Outlook, other contact programs, or other Webmail accounts. By populating your Connections from the start with a good number of contacts from your current address book, you can quickly see how LinkedIn works and might benefit you.

Begin by clicking on the "Add Connections" item under the Contacts menu option (see Figure 4.1 above) or the link in the top right corner of any LinkedIn page. On the left of your screen will be a large box with the title "See Who You Already Know on LinkedIn" (see Figure 4.2). There is a link to "Learn More" for additional help, but it is not difficult to figure out what to do.

Figure 4.2: Add Connections Menu

Your first choice, if you have a Webmail account (e.g., Gmail or Hotmail), is to enter your e-mail address and password. LinkedIn will not store your password or send out any e-mail from your account. It will import your contacts so you can see them on LinkedIn.

Your second choice, and the one that will apply to many lawyers who use Outlook in their practices, is to import your Outlook contacts. There is a link at the bottom of the box labeled "Import your desktop contacts." You can also import contacts from Apple Mail and other e-mail applications, but we will use Outlook as our example (see Figure 4.3).

Figure 4.3: Importing Desktop E-mail Contacts

When you click on that link, you will move to a screen that asks you to choose and upload a file with your contacts. What file, you might ask?

It is best to prepare to import your Outlook contacts in advance and create the file you want to upload. Although the steps vary in each version of Outlook, simply search for "exporting contacts" in the Outlook Help menu, which will bring up step-by-step directions through this process.

There are two important things to remember. First, you will want to export your contacts in the comma-separated values (.csv) format. When prompted in Outlook for a format, choose "Comma-separated values (Windows)." Second, create a logical name for the file (e.g., contacts.csv) and remember where you save it.

Once you create the .csv file of your contacts, go back to LinkedIn and the "Import your desktop contacts" link, click it, choose the .csv file you created as the file to upload, and upload the file (see Figure 4.4). LinkedIn again reminds you that it will not send e-mails to your contacts.

Figure 4.4: Uploading CSV File

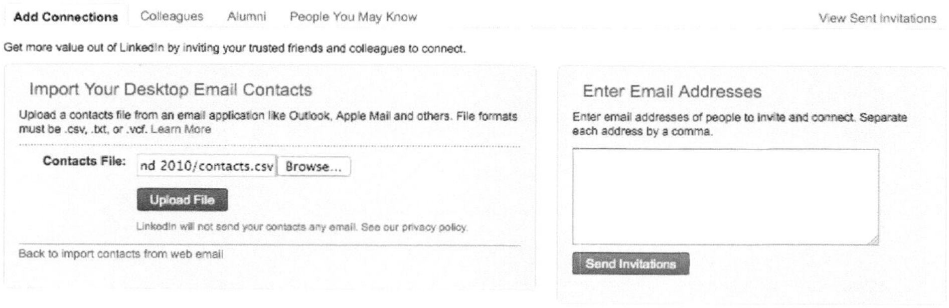

It can take a few minutes to upload and process your contacts file, especially if you have a lot of contacts. Once the process is completed, you will see all of your Outlook contacts inside LinkedIn arranged alphabetically, with a separate list for each letter (see Figure 4.5).

Figure 4.5: Imported Contacts Results

Each imported contact will have a checkbox in front of the name, and some will have a small LinkedIn "in" logo after the name. The LinkedIn logo means that the person is already a LinkedIn user. People already on LinkedIn obviously are more likely to add you as a Connection than people who are not already on LinkedIn.

To invite people into your Connections, simply check the box in front the name. The name of the person will appear in a list on the right of the page (see Figure 4.6). Pick the people you want to invite,

Figure 4.6: Inviting Imported Contacts

click on the link to send the invitations, and wait to receive notifications from the people who have accepted your invitations.

This importing technique is a simple and powerful way to add new Connections or to update your current list of Connections. As of the time this book was written, this approach has one drawback. In the past, you could send a customized invitation to the people you invited. Now, you can only send a generic invitation. Personalized invitations are always the preferred approach. Your best contacts might not appreciate a generic approach, and other contacts might not remember who you are.

Method 2: Connecting with Colleagues and Former Colleagues

Current and former colleagues are an important source of Connections. As a result, LinkedIn makes it very easy to find colleagues and add them as Connections if you complete your Profile with all the places you have worked. LinkedIn will automatically supply a list of potential Connections from those places.

Go to the Contacts menu and click on "Add Contacts." LinkedIn will take you to the "Add Connections" page, and you will see a tab for "Colleagues" (see Figure 4.7).

Figure 4.7: Colleagues Tab

Click on "Colleagues." You will see a list of organizations you listed on your Profile, including where you currently work and all the other places you have worked in the past (see Figure 4.8). For each organization, you will find a button to "view all" of the contacts on

31

Figure 4.8: Colleagues List

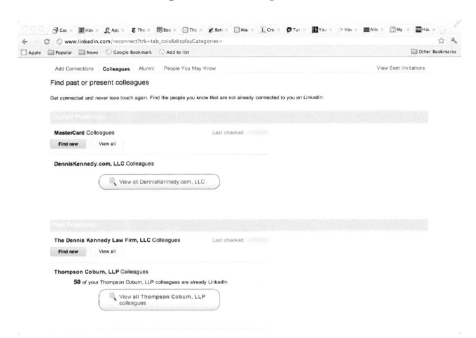

LinkedIn who have identified in their Profiles that they also worked at those organizations.

Click on the "view all" button to see a box with a list of names of LinkedIn members who have listed that organization on their Profiles and check boxes in front of those names (see Figure 4.9). Click on a name to view the person's Profile. Click on the check boxes in front of the names to add those names to a box on the right to whom you can send invitations.

Under the invitation box, you can personalize the invitation you send or use a generic invitation. We always recommend that you personalize, even if you invite a large number of people. Saying something as simple as "Have great memories of the days we spent as associates at ABC Firm" will help people remember you and make them more likely to add you as a Connection and to reply to you personally.

Figure 4.9: Colleague Results

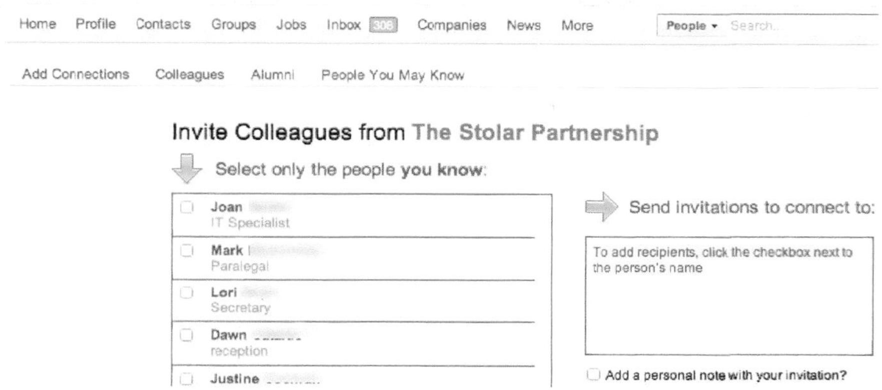

Method 3: Connecting with Alumni

LinkedIn has also determined that the people you went to school with will be another rich and common source of contacts for most people, especially for lawyers. The Alumni feature works the same way as the Colleagues feature.

Go to the Contacts menu and click on "Add Contacts." Then, click on the tab for "Alumni" to see a list of the schools that you attended, which you included on your Profile (see Figure 4.10).

Figure 4.10: Alumni Submenu

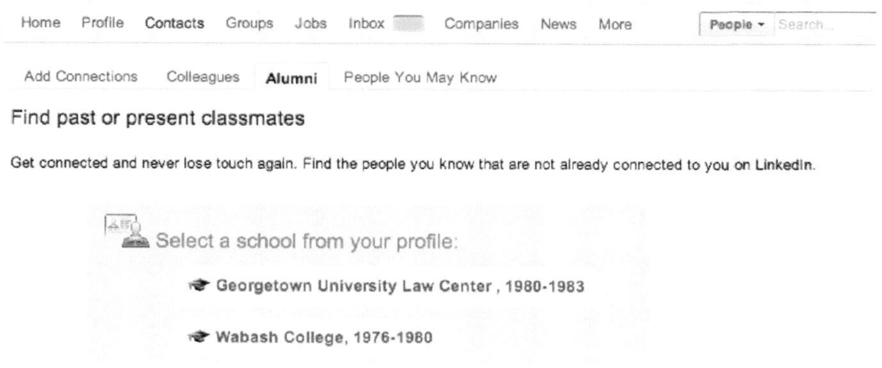

For each school, you can click on the school's name to bring up a screen with demographic and other information about your class and a list of classmates already on LinkedIn who have identified in their Profiles that they also attended the school (see Figure 4.11). A great feature is that you can view a list of people who graduated the same year you did or who attended the school in any of the years you did. You can refine your search by where they work, what they do, or where they live. Click on the "Connect" button for anyone that you would like to invite to be a Connection.

Figure 4.11: Alumni Results

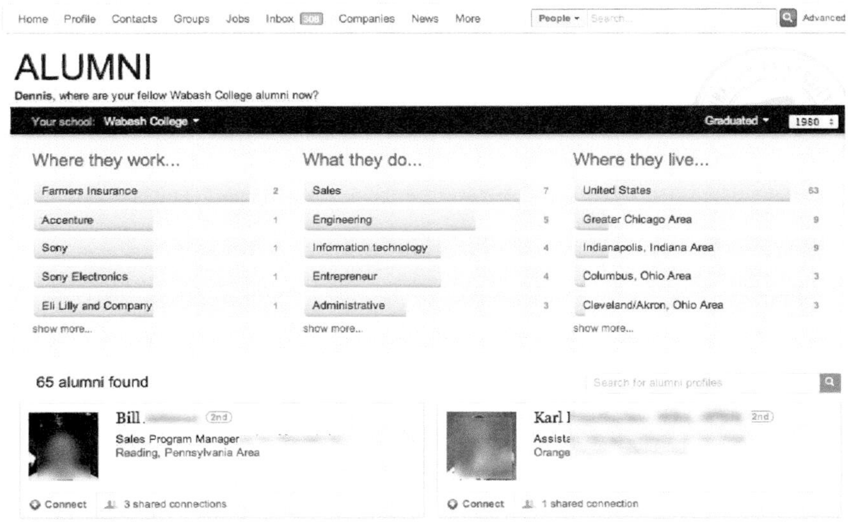

As in the case of Colleagues, you can personalize the invitation you send or use a generic invitation. Of course, you will want to personalize to help people remember you and make them more likely to add you as a Connection.

These three tools will get you off to a great start. You should already be getting the idea that there is no excuse for having only a tiny number of Connections on LinkedIn. In the next Lesson, we show five more tools to build your network of Connections.

Making Even More Connections

In Lesson 4, we showed you three fast and powerful ways to build your network of Connections. In this Lesson, we discuss five more connecting techniques and highlight the importance of treating the development of your Connection list as an evolving process that you should pay attention to on a regular basis.

Once again, we will be focusing primarily on the "Contacts" menu and the "Add Connections" submenu under that for most of these methods (see Figure 5.1).

Figure 5.1: Add Connections

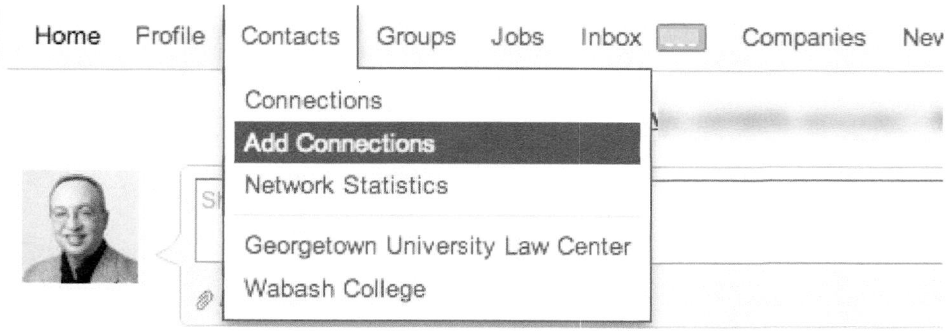

Method 1: People You May Know

A great way to add Connections that works better the more you use LinkedIn is the "People You May Know" tool. LinkedIn "learns" from your Connections, your Connections' Connections, and your LinkedIn usage. It then suggests people to whom you might wish to connect. There are times when the suggestions can be eerily accurate. Most of the time you check this tool, you will find at least one suggestion of a person who it really does make sense to add as a Connection.

The "People You May Know" tool is another tab choice under "Add Connections" like "Colleagues" and "Alumni" (see Figure 5.2).

Figure 5.2: "People You May Know" Tab

Clicking on this link brings up a list of people LinkedIn thinks you might know and the number of Connections you have in common, with a button you can click to connect (see Figure 5.3). It also offers you the chance to personalize your invitations.

Figure 5.3: "People You May Know" Results

On your Homepage (discussed in Lesson 9), you will also see a box highlighting suggestions and a link to People You May Know.

Method 2: Invitations from Individual's Profiles

There are many ways, inside and outside LinkedIn, to find a LinkedIn user's Profile. We will discuss search tools in more detail in Lesson 6 and in the Advanced Topics section; however, not surprisingly, you can use LinkedIn's search features to find individuals. You will also find that people will provide links to their LinkedIn Profiles on their Web sites or blogs. For many people, their LinkedIn Profiles will be on the first page of results in a Google search on their name.

No matter what route you take, once you reach someone's LinkedIn Profile, you will find three ways to contact them or add them as a Connection (see Figure 5.4).

Figure 5.4: Profile Example

First, you can contact the person by e-mail through the LinkedIn system using a feature called InMail. This e-mail is routed through LinkedIn and not your normal e-mail system. Note that some organizations block this feature for employees using work computers.

Second, you can request an introduction through someone else connected to the person with whom you want to connect. As we have mentioned, LinkedIn works on the principles of "six degrees of separation." Someone directly connected to you is a first-level Connection. Someone connected to your first-level Connection (but not directly to you) is a second-level Connection. You will also find third-level Connections (someone connected to a second-level Connection of yours). When you reach someone's Profile, LinkedIn will display what level Connection you are with a blue circle (see Figure 5.4, where the blue circle to the right of Kevin Bacon's name indicates that he is a second-level Connection).

In general, it is easy to communicate with and through first-level Connections. As you move out in Connections, it takes an "introduction" to move between levels, much like in the real world. By requesting an introduction, you ask one of your first-level Connections to send an introduction to one of their first-level Connections asking that they add you as a Connection. Again, you definitely want to personalize your message when making a request (see Figure 5.5).

Figure 5.5: Introduction Request

Third, you can send an invitation directly to people by clicking the "Connect" button. You will then see a menu giving you options to classify the way you might know the person (see Figure 5.6). These include colleague, classmate, done business together, friend, or other. Some of the categories require that you input the person's e-mail to send an invitation. Take care in using this option and make sure that you send a personalized invitation so the person you invite remembers you.

Figure 5.6: Invitation Options

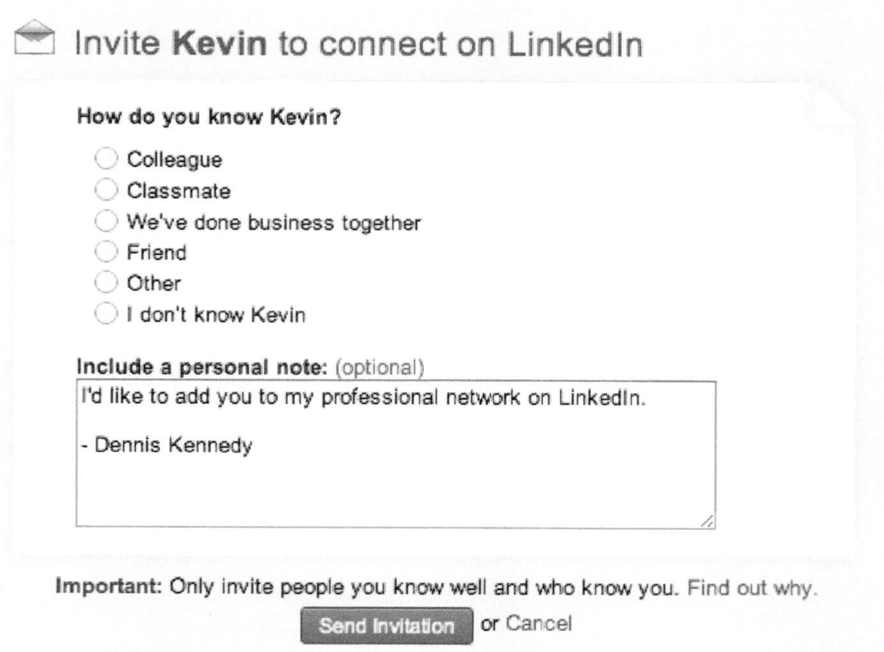

✉ Invite **Kevin** to connect on LinkedIn

How do you know Kevin?

○ Colleague
○ Classmate
○ We've done business together
○ Friend
○ Other
○ I don't know Kevin

Include a personal note: (optional)

I'd like to add you to my professional network on LinkedIn.

- Dennis Kennedy

Important: Only invite people you know well and who know you. Find out why.

[Send Invitation] or Cancel

Be aware that this feature can cause a lot of confusion, depending on the category you select. A generic invitation that says only that the person "did business together" with you is not likely to get a response unless the person actually remembers you.

Method 3: Accepting Invitations

Do not forget this obvious way to add Connections. You undoubtedly received e-mails with LinkedIn invitations before you became a LinkedIn user and after you set up your account. You will find that, on a fairly regular basis, you will get invitations to connect to others. You can receive those invitations in your LinkedIn Inbox, through an e-mail notification, or by both methods.

When you get an invitation, even from someone you know well, do not simply click on the "accept invitation" link in the e-mail. Instead, go to the inviter's Profile page and confirm who they are, see what they are doing, and view in particular the shared Connections you have. You can learn some valuable information about relationships within your network. If you are not sure who someone is, seeing who else they are connected to can help you determine whether to add them. You might also use the contact information on the person's Profile to e-mail them to ask them how you know each other and why you might want to connect.

If you know the person or want to engage them in conversation, we recommend answering the invitation with an e-mail thanking them for the Connection and adding some personal comments. If you do not know the person and do not want them to contact you again, you can click on the "I don't know this person" button in the invitation.

Method 4: Drawing from Your Groups

As you become involved with LinkedIn, you are likely to join Groups, which we discuss in more detail in Lesson 7. Groups can be a source of Connections, especially as you learn more about people and engage in discussions with them. LinkedIn makes it easy to invite other members of a Group you join to become a Connection.

Method 5: In-person Meetings

For many years, it was a source of frustration that you could meet some-one in person and exchange business cards, but had a difficult process of adding them as a Connection because they were not first-level Connections. LinkedIn recognized and addressed this problem in its mobile apps. In the older versions of the various LinkedIn mobile apps (iPhone, Android, BlackBerry), there was a feature called "In Person" that allowed you and someone you met in person to immediately connect using your mobile phones, even though you were not first-level Connections.

As of this writing, the "In Person" feature is not part of the LinkedIn app (discussed in more detail in Lesson 9). Instead, you can use a LinkedIn app called CardMunch, which is free and available through the applicable app store (currently only for Apple iOS devices, but this might have changed by the time you read this). It uses the camera in your smartphone to let you take a picture of someone's business card. The picture is uploaded and transcribed for you. You can add that contact information to your Outlook or other contacts application or directly invite the person to connect with you on LinkedIn without an introduction from a go-between.

Connecting Is an Ongoing Process

You can see that LinkedIn offers easy, powerful tools to get your network off to a fast start and include people who really should be added to your network. However, do not stop after you first use these tools. You will continue to meet people. People will want to connect with you. Your networks, both online and real world, will continue to grow and evolve. We recommend that you set aside a little time several times a year to use some of these methods to update your LinkedIn network and make it even more valuable to you.

Our advice is to start building your network with people you know reasonably well and to whom you want to be connected, and learn to work on LinkedIn with those Connections. Then, gradually grow your network of Connections in an organic way, much as you do in the real world. Your approach and the number of Connections in your networks will vary. As an example, Dennis has well over one thousand Connections, but that does not mean that is a good number for you. Many of his Connections come from his writing and speaking audiences and, most importantly, he has been on LinkedIn for more than eight years, slowly adding Connections by using the techniques we discussed in this and the previous Lesson.

Now that you have some Connections, we look at some of the ways you can search, filter, and use Connections on LinkedIn in Lesson 6.

Using LinkedIn Search

Once you have uploaded your contacts and have begun sending (and accepting) invitations to connect on LinkedIn, it is time to begin using LinkedIn as a tool to build your practice and broaden your network. Aside from job hunting, professionals use LinkedIn mostly for keeping in touch, industry networking, and promoting their business. As a result, LinkedIn contains a potential goldmine of information and potential contacts.

Use LinkedIn's robust search engine to find potential future Connections or to identify potential clients, referral sources, and industry contacts.

How to Get Started Finding People

Searching by Name

The easiest way to begin looking for people is by searching their name. Type the name into the "quick search" box at the upper-right corner of the page on LinkedIn (see Figure 6.1).

Figure 6.1: Quick Search

As you type, LinkedIn will begin giving you "suggestions" that will appear under the search box (see Figure 6.2). If you see the person you are searching for in the list of suggestions, use your mouse to scroll down and click directly on that person. (If you cannot see the drop-down list of suggestions when you use the quick search box, check to be sure that suggestions are "turned on" at the bottom of the drop-down box.)

Figure 6.2: Suggestions

If you do not use the suggestions LinkedIn provides in the drop-down box, continue typing and then click Enter (or click on the magnifying glass to the right of the search box). You will obtain results only for the category you searched under (i.e., if you are searching People, you will only get results for People, not Companies, Groups, etc.).

To begin building your network, search *anyone*—friends, colleagues, classmates, neighbors, former colleagues, supervisors, sports teammates, church congregation, etc. Some of those people might have been in your contact database that you have uploaded to LinkedIn, but others might not have been.

Searching Existing Connections for New Contacts

As we discussed in Lesson 4, LinkedIn's Contacts menu helps you connect with some of your existing contacts, including Alumni and Colleagues. You can expand your network by searching their individual Profiles for new Connections.

Is someone in your list of contacts a master networker or particularly well connected? Navigate to their Profile on LinkedIn. Scroll down the page and look for the module on the right side that reads, "[First name]'s Connections." You will see a partial list of that individual's Connections, beginning with your shared Connections (see Figure 6.3).

Because you are already connected to your shared Connections, click on "See all Connections" at the bottom of the box. LinkedIn will take you to a new screen that lists all of that individual's Connections (unless they have established privacy settings to hide them; we will discuss privacy settings in Lesson 10). Now you can see whether your Contact is connected to other people that you already know (but have not yet connected with on LinkedIn), or whether they have some Connections to whom you would like to be introduced.

Figure 6.3: Profile Page Showing Connections

Other Searches

As you may have guessed, you can also use the drop-down menu on the quick search box to search Companies, Groups, Answers, Updates, or Jobs (see Figure 6.4). If you do not have a specific name, you can search by keyword, school, or other parameters using this search box as well.

Regardless of the category you choose from the quick search drop-down box, once you type in your search terms, you will receive suggestions categorized by Connections, Companies, Groups, and now even Skills (see Figure 6.5).

You can easily see which of your Connections (first- or second-level) has a particular skill or keyword in his or her Profile, which Groups discuss the items about which you are interested in learning, and which Companies match those keyword terms. Click on any of these categories for more information.

Figure 6.4: Quick Search Options

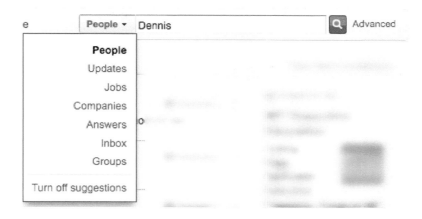

Figure 6.5: Quick Search Suggestions

47

For example, if you click on any of the suggestions in the Skills category, you will be taken to a new page (see Figure 6.6) that indicates the primary industry to which that skill relates, along with:

- A definition of the Skill (from Wikipedia)
- A list of professionals who include that Skill in their Profiles
- Information about your level of Connection to that individual
- A list of related Skills
- A list of Groups that relate to that Skill
- Trends related to that Skill

Figure 6.6: Skills Result—Trial Advocacy

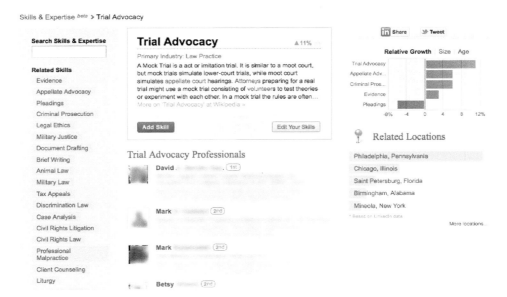

This technique might help you find experts or other specialists.

By contrast, clicking directly on a Company (rather than an individual) in the quick search suggestion list will bring you to that Company's Overview page (see Figure 6.7), which includes a brief company description and a listing of those in your network, as well as a full list of

Figure 6.7: Company Overview Page

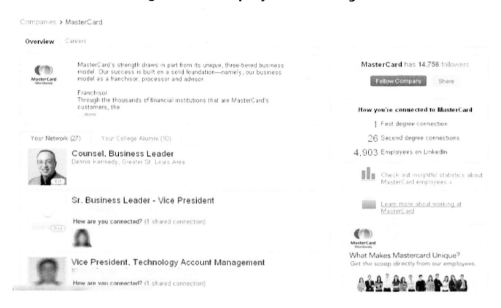

employees and how you are connected to them. For more on searching Companies, see the Advanced Search Features section in the Advanced Topics section of this book.

Taking Advantage of the Power of LinkedIn Search

LinkedIn is filled with high-level business professionals who use it specifically for business networking. Some of these people you might know or have had contact with in the past, but lost touch. Others might be people you want to know or who could be the key to bringing in a new account, but in the past, you had no way "in." LinkedIn might be the key to finding your way in.

One of the best ways to establish yourself as a trusted advisor is to show an interest in and get to know your clients, their businesses, and their challenges. Searching for information on LinkedIn is an excellent way to find out what clients, potential clients, referral sources, and industry experts are talking about and what they think is important. Let this information inform your marketing efforts and your marketing message, including your activity on LinkedIn.

To obtain more information about clients or their industry, view not only their Web site, but also their LinkedIn Company Page and individual LinkedIn Profile. Impress potential clients from the beginning and demonstrate the kind of personal attention you will provide them by researching them before your first meeting.

Search is an excellent tool to get competitive intelligence about what your competitors and competitors' clients are doing. In addition, we discuss the unique value LinkedIn search brings to the hiring process in the Advanced Topics section of this book, as well as even more search features. Are you beginning to see the value of using LinkedIn search? Let us now move to Lesson 7 to get started in actually participating on LinkedIn.

Participating on LinkedIn Using Updates and Groups

You have created your Profile; uploaded your Contacts; invited friends, co-workers, colleagues, and referral sources to connect; and sought out new avenues of business. Now is not the time to sit back and wait for LinkedIn invitations to arrive in your e-mail inbox!

The third essential building block of effective LinkedIn use is Participation. After all, it is the essence of networking. Whether you are already "connected" to your target audience or not, you must nurture these relationships and get active.

To be effective, you must do more than just show up. The real value of any networking site is to build real, genuine relationships with the other people on the network who are in your target audience, whether that target audience is your potential clients, referral sources, or strategic alliances.

Conventional marketing wisdom says it usually takes anywhere from seven to twelve "touches" before someone will do business with you. Those "touches" can include e-mail, in-person contacts, advertisements, direct referrals, articles, and the like. Even when someone does business with you or refers a client for the first time, however, it is not over. You must still remain memorable so that he or she continues to do so. Posting Updates and participating in Groups are great ways to communicate to your network on an ongoing basis and keep your name at the forefront of your target audience.

Let us begin with Updates.

Updates

Updates are short messages you share with your network, similar to Facebook status updates or Twitter tweets. Share Updates with your network directly from your LinkedIn Home page using the update box (see Figure 7.1).

Figure 7.1: Updates Box

LinkedIn status Updates are limited to 140 characters—the same limit that applies to a single tweet on Twitter. Think of Updates as very short marketing or networking messages. Keep them professional. Do not be too self-promotional.

What to Include in a LinkedIn Update

Some Updates should be about you and your practice, but other Updates can focus more on your audience. Use the "so what" test when composing Updates: ask yourself why your network would care about what you have to say. Think about how it relates to *them* and their business. Observe carefully what others in your network do well and try to adopt a similar approach.

Some ideas for LinkedIn Updates include:

- If you have your own blog, provide the title of a recent post with a shortened URL link (from TinyURL or Bit.ly)
- Link to an article you read that might be of interest to your network, especially if it relates to your practice area, local community, or your clients' industry
- Post a brief note about a recent court decision, new regulation, or news story relevant to your area of practice
- Link to a short YouTube video that can provide value to your network
- Write an important announcement or news item about you or your firm (this also can be a great cross-selling tool)
- Link to an article in which you are quoted; include the publication, article title, and a short description (if space allows)
- Link to an event or industry conference you are attending (or simply include the fact of your attendance in your Update)

Although many people link their Twitter accounts to LinkedIn, we do not recommend doing so unless your tweets are purely professional and are not part of a conversation. Your LinkedIn Updates should stand alone and, more importantly, should provide value to your network.

Why Post LinkedIn Updates?

If your Updates provide value to others, they can be powerful PR and brand-building tools. Your network will begin to look to you and your Updates as a valuable source of information, in turn building your expert status.

When you post an Update on LinkedIn, it will appear on the Home page of each of your Connections (although the more Connections they have, and the more active those Connections are, the less likely they will see any one specific Update on their Home page). Your Connections will also receive your Updates when LinkedIn sends its weekly "Network Update" e-mail. Your latest status update is always displayed on your LinkedIn Profile. However, you will not see your own Updates in the "Network Update" e-mail you receive from LinkedIn; you will see only the Updates posted by your Connections.

Networking is not a one-way street; when you receive Network Updates by e-mail or on your LinkedIn Home page, take note of the Updates posted by others in your network. Occasionally, send notes in response via InMail, e-mail, or regular mail or give them a call.

Groups

One of the best ways to build stronger relationships within LinkedIn is through Groups. There are LinkedIn Groups organized around almost any topic you can think of: alumni, industries, practice areas, hobbies, and many more. If you cannot find a Group to suit your needs or interests, you can start your own. Find the Groups tab on the main LinkedIn navigation bar (see Figure 7.2).

Figure 7.2: Groups Menu

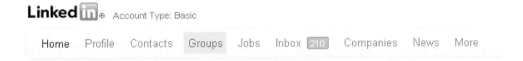

Finding Groups to Join
Search Groups for your target market, your industry, your clients' industries, your practice areas, or your alma mater. To make it even easier, search for Groups to which you already belong offline. Many bar associations, lawyers groups, and community groups have corresponding LinkedIn Groups.

Go to the Groups tab on the main LinkedIn navigation bar and click on "Groups You May Like" (see Figure 7.3).

Figure 7.3: "Groups You May Like" Submenu

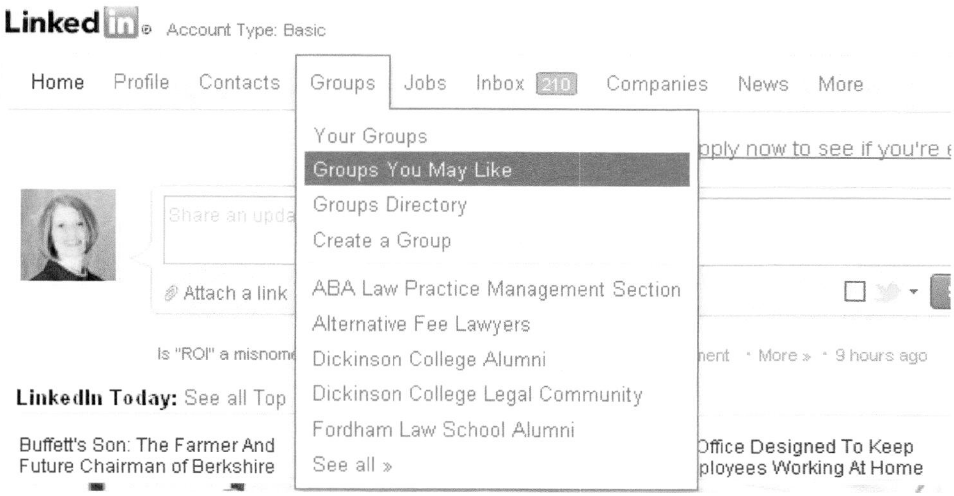

Choose Groups that are big enough to have depth, but small enough to allow you to be visible and to actively contribute.

Some Groups will allow you to join immediately, whereas others are moderated Groups where you must "apply" to be accepted into the Group. Groups are moderated to ensure that the messages and participation will not include spam and that a prospective member is someone who legitimately should be part of the Group.

To receive the most benefit from Groups, you must be an active participant—that means discussing, writing, commenting, and connecting with Group members. When you participate, other Group members will see your picture and a mini-Profile including your name and headline on which they can click to see your full Profile.

What to Do in Groups

We suggest that you choose a few Groups that especially appeal to you and in which you likely will become active. Avoid spreading yourself too thin and feeling overwhelmed. Although you can join several Groups, the better approach is to simply monitor most of them as they interest you first before becoming an active participant.

Begin by viewing the discussions and contributing where you can add value. Look for "most popular" discussions as a good place to start your Group participation. You can find them under the Discussions tab for each Group.

Once you get a feel for the Group culture, you can begin posting your own discussions, which may include linking back to content on your Web site or blog. Be sure the content you post and to which you link is appropriate for the Group and is not just a sales pitch.

Share or "like" discussions from your Groups with the rest of your network. This is part of the "karma" of LinkedIn (and of all good networking)—give before you receive. Sharing others' work brings them visibility; eventually, it will come back to you. People will seek out opportunities to reciprocate.

The Benefits of Groups

In Groups, people share information, brainstorm ideas, discuss their interests and challenges, and post informational articles or links, making it easy for you to get to know others and for them to get to know you.

Groups can provide fodder for your other online activities—blog posts, tweets, etc.—to create a fully integrated online marketing presence. Get ideas from Groups containing your target market about what they are interested in, what their concerns are, and what services might be helpful to them just by watching the discussion.

When you join a Group, you can see the list of members, making it easy to identify people with particular interests or challenges and to navigate to their Profiles for more information. You will also see who the influencers are—those who participate regularly, whose advice others seek in the Group, and who provide great answers or provoke interesting discussions.

Another advantage to belonging to Groups is that you can easily add other Group members as Connections; LinkedIn allows fellow Group members to send invitations without having any additional information, such as an e-mail address. Once you are connected to another Group member, it is much easier to communicate with that person directly.

Active participation in Groups helps you become known as a subject matter expert. Your Updates to your network can establish you as someone who shares valuable content, but Groups takes that one step further. In Group discussions you have more "real estate" to demonstrate your knowledge and provide real help and information-packed content. And best of all, when you participate in Group discussions, you reach beyond your direct network Connections.

Start Your Own Group

Although it is a good idea to get involved in an existing Group, especially when starting out on LinkedIn, there are good reasons for starting your own Group (if you are up to it). It can be difficult to get a new Group started, but if you think your Group has something different to offer, you might think it worthwhile. For example, we started a Group in connection with this book for readers. You must do a lot of work up front to get a Group going. Invite your Connections to join the Group, for example. Our advice is to focus on bringing people together who can benefit from sharing mutual experiences and insights. Start some discussions. Ask others to participate by starting or joining in on existing discussions.

Just because there is one Group on a particular subject does not mean that there cannot be others. You will want to see what is going on in the other Groups first and determine whether it makes sense to be there or to create your own space with your own audience. You might create a Group with a local focus or narrow a specific topic to carve out your own space. It really does come down to answering the question: "What do you want?" In addition, it is difficult to overestimate how much time and effort it might take to promote your Group and get it to a point of critical mass.

Updates and Groups are just two of the participation tools available on LinkedIn. For more ways to participate, let us move to Lesson 8, where we discuss Answers and Recommendations.

Benefiting from LinkedIn Answers and Recommendations

Active LinkedIn users take advantage of two other powerful techniques to enhance their reputation and increase the value they provide to their networks, as well as the value of their networks to their Connections. These techniques are Answers and Recommendations, and they work much as they do in the real world.

LinkedIn Answers

LinkedIn's Answers is a question-and-answer tool and is organized by category. Think of Answers as a corollary to discussions in Groups, but the potential audience is LinkedIn as a whole, rather than just the single Group of which you are a member. Answers are another place to showcase your expertise, but here you can also find answers to questions that may have already been faced by others or identify industry and thought leaders with whom to connect.

Getting Started with Answers

Answers can be found under the "More" tab to the extreme right of the LinkedIn navigation bar (see Figure 8.1).

Figure 8.1: More Submenu—Answers

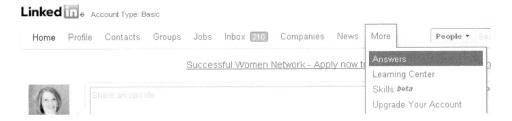

Clicking on Answers will take you to the Answers Homepage (see Figure 8.2).

Figure 8.2: Answers Homepage

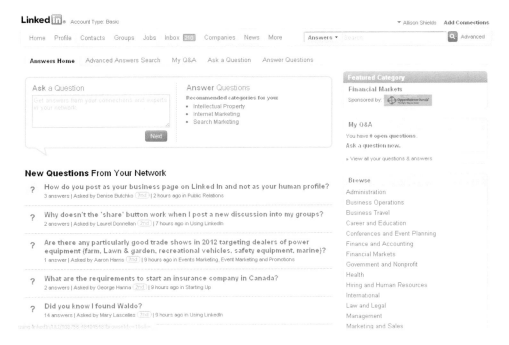

To get a feel for questions and answers on LinkedIn, begin by searching topics related to your practice areas or your clients' industries using the now-familiar quick search box. Enter keywords or questions you are frequently asked by prospects or new clients. Alternatively, browse Answers by topic in the right sidebar on the Answers Homepage. You can also simply review new questions posted by people in your network on the Answers Homepage.

You can also search Answers using the Advanced Answers search tab, which will give you a matrix with the ability to filter your search results and even show only questions that have not yet been answered.

Answering Questions

Under the "Answer Questions" tab, you may view open questions, closed questions (answers no longer being accepted), or "Experts." Viewing "Experts" will show those people categorized by LinkedIn as experts. According to LinkedIn:

> Earn expertise by answering questions asked by other LinkedIn professionals. When your answer is chosen as best by the question's asker, you gain a point of expertise in the question's category.

You can build your reputation as an expert by answering questions, particularly if your answers are chosen as the "best answers."

Asking Questions

At the top of the Answers Homepage, you will see a box in which to type a question. Next to that, LinkedIn will suggest categories for you to answer others' questions based on your LinkedIn activity. Click on the topic to view questions asked in those categories.

You can also ask questions by navigating to the "Ask a Question" tab. Here you can add details and categories and indicate whether your question has a geographical component.

The "My Q&A" tab under Answers lets you keep track of your activity by showing you the questions you have asked and the answers you have given to others.

Answers Tips

- Keep Answers professional
- Do not use Answers as a billboard or a place to post your advertisements
- Do not start selling before you build trust and relationships with your network and Connections
- Do not just answer questions with an offer of a consultation or an exhortation to visit your Web site
- Include links to blog posts related to the question
- Give step-by-step instructions for solving the issue
- Direct users to e-books or other free resources on your Web site

Be mindful of the applicable ethical rules when answering questions or participating in Groups. Two big concerns are inadvertently establishing a lawyer-client relationship and whether you are giving legal advice with your answer or comment. We discuss some of the major ethical issues in using LinkedIn in the Advanced Topics section of this book.

Recommendations

Recommendations are just what you would expect: a way for clients, colleagues, employers, co-workers, referral sources, and strategic alliances to recommend your work, or for you to recommend theirs. They are essentially testimonials that appear on a LinkedIn Profile. Remember that LinkedIn considers Recommendations when deciding the completeness of your Profile. However, LinkedIn Recommendations do raise issues about "endorsements" under ethical rules. See the ethics discussion in the Advanced Topics section of this book.

You can find Recommendations under the Profile tab on the main LinkedIn navigation bar (see Figure 8.3).

When you click on Recommendations, you will be taken to a page that shows the Recommendations you have received from others (if

Figure 8.3: Profile Submenu—Recommendations

any), organized by position and school. Below that, you will be given the option to make a Recommendation.

Recommending Others

Writing a Recommendation for another professional (even when they do not ask) is a good way to express your appreciation for a job well done or to give back. To make a Recommendation, choose someone from your contact list or enter his or her name and e-mail address, and then choose the category for which you wish to recommend him or her (Colleague, Service Provider, etc.). Then click "continue," and LinkedIn will walk you through the quick and easy Recommendation process.

Once your Recommendation has been completed, LinkedIn will notify the other person of your Recommendation, who will be asked to approve or reject it. LinkedIn allows only approved Recommendations to appear on your Profile.

When you recommend someone else, your comment is also listed on your Profile in the right sidebar under "[Your Name] Recommends." This provides additional value to those whom you recommend because people viewing your Profile will be "introduced" to them through your Profile. You can write a Recommendation for any professional, even if they are not on LinkedIn.

Getting Recommended

Recommendations are useful for all of the same reasons testimonials are useful. What a third party says about you is always more valuable than what you say about yourself. Recommendations can highlight specific aspects of your service or tell a story about what it is like to work with you. And, according to LinkedIn, users with Recommendations are three times as likely to get inquiries through LinkedIn searches as those with no Recommendations.

Recommendations you receive are listed under "Recommendations For" at the bottom of the "Experience" section or "School" to which the Recommendation relates. They are also listed in a separate "Recommendations" section on your Profile.

You can request Recommendations only from your Connections. If you would like to request a Recommendation, go to the Request Recommendations tab (see Figure 8.4), enter the position or school for which you would like to receive the Recommendation, enter the person from whom you are requesting the Recommendation, and then create your request message.

Figure 8.4: Request Recommendations Tab

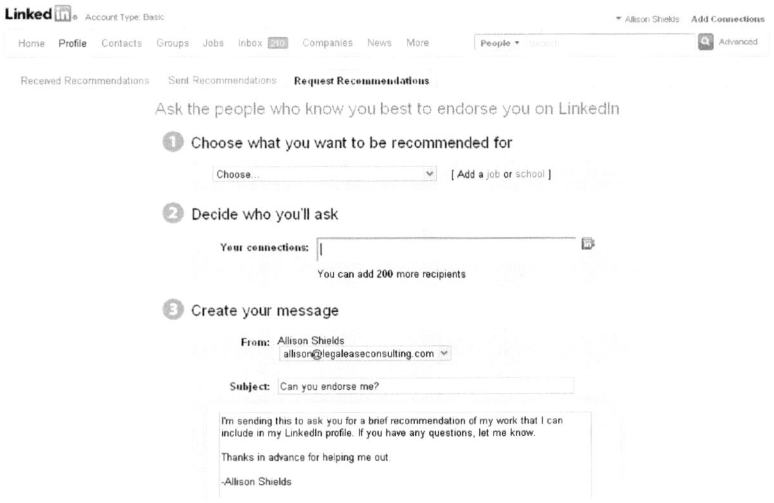

Recommendation Request Tips

- Send Recommendation requests individually, rather than in bulk
- Do not rely on the stock message created by LinkedIn
- Customize the request for each recipient
- Ask for a recommendation on a specific project or request that your Connection discuss a specific aspect of your service, your approach, or your skills
- When you receive a nice compliment from one of your Connections outside of LinkedIn, ask them if they would mind posting their comments as a Recommendation on LinkedIn and send them a request
- If you are concerned about receiving Recommendations from clients, ask for Recommendations from referral sources, colleagues, co-workers, or others who are familiar with your work
- Request Recommendations from other organizations where you are active: charitable boards, local bar associations, volunteer or community groups, etc.
- Ensure you review and approve Recommendations your Connections make and request revisions where necessary.

Now that you are participating on LinkedIn, let us learn how you can monitor that activity and the activity of those in your network in Lesson 9.

Monitoring Your Network

Home   Profile   Contacts   Groups   Jobs   Inbox ▭   Companies   News   More   People ▾ | Search...

In many ways, LinkedIn simply transplants what you do with your real-world network into an Internet service. In this Lesson, we discuss something great real-world networkers do well: monitor their networks and keep track of what is going on with their Connections. LinkedIn makes it easy for you to do what the best real-world networkers work very hard to accomplish.

Great real-world networkers have an uncanny ability to know what is happening in their networks. They seem to know who moved to another firm before anyone else does, who is looking for a new job, who has won an award, and who has had other news. They also know who in their network is working with someone else in the network (perhaps because they facilitated that engagement) and who should be meeting someone else. In other words, they have a great sense of community.

For these people, obtaining this information seems effortless and second nature. For the rest of us, we wonder how they find any time to work given how much time they must spend keeping up with goings-on in their networks.

LinkedIn gives each of us tools to monitor what is happening in our networks in simple yet comprehensive ways so that we each can have the kind of "eyes and ears" that the best real-world networkers have. In fact, using LinkedIn, you can keep up with your network in just a few minutes daily or weekly.

We will cover three effective ways you can monitor your LinkedIn network: the LinkedIn Homepage, e-mail notifications, and the LinkedIn mobile app.

Method 1: The LinkedIn Homepage

When you log into your LinkedIn account, your LinkedIn Homepage appears. LinkedIn has made many improvements to the Homepage over the years, and now it is quite good. In one convenient page or "dashboard," you have easy access to LinkedIn features and information about what is happening in your LinkedIn world (see Figure 9.1).

Figure 9.1: LinkedIn Homepage

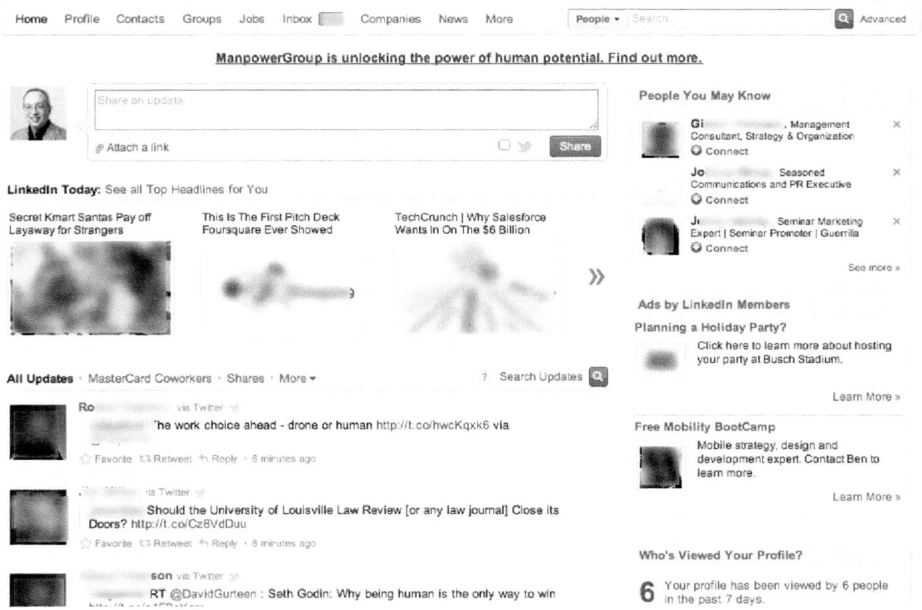

Across the top, you will find the tabbed menus taking you to the features we discussed in the previous Lessons. Among these tabs is your Inbox, with a number indicating how many new invitations and messages are waiting for you. On the top right, the search box is available.

Below the tabs on the left is "LinkedIn Today," a set of links to news and other items shared by your Connections that LinkedIn's algorithms think you will find interesting. The theory, of course, is that you will probably be interested in what your Connections find interesting.

Below LinkedIn Today is a list, in reverse chronological order, of the latest updates from your Connections. These might include Profile changes, Updates about what they are doing, tweets automatically reposted from Twitter, and other news and information. In a few minutes a day, you can monitor your network in one convenient place.

Below the Updates, LinkedIn lets you see people in your Colleagues and Alumni categories who have recently joined LinkedIn (see Figure 9.2). Click on the links and determine whether you might add people you know as Connections.

Figure 9.2: "Just Joined LinkedIn" Options

Ja   Bryan Johnson is returning from a trip to Orlando, FL., via Tripit
http://ow.ly/1ge7wG
Like · Comment · Send a message · Share · 1 hour ago

Show more...

Just joined LinkedIn

Colleagues
MasterCard
DennisKennedy.com, LLC
The Dennis Kennedy Law Firm, LLC
Thompson Coburn, LLP
NetTech, Inc.
The Stolar Partnership

Alumni
Georgetown University Law Center
Wabash College

On the upper-right column below the search box, you will find a section for People You May Know—another way to easily add Connections we discussed in Lesson 5. Below that, you can learn who has viewed your Profile (or at least a limited number of them; to get more you will need a premium account), the current number of people in your network, Groups you might join, Companies you might want to follow, and Events in your network.

As you can see, the Homepage can be a powerful and convenient monitoring tool that will help you keep up with what is happening in your network. Spending a few minutes a day or a few times a week will level the playing field with the best real-world networkers.

Method 2: E-mail and RSS Notifications

Can you stand any more e-mails? If you can, you can receive e-mail notifications about happenings in your LinkedIn network without the need to go to your LinkedIn Homepage on a regular basis. As we discuss in Lesson 10, you can simply set up the e-mail notifications you want under your account settings. Once you have configured your e-mail notifications, you will receive e-mails from LinkedIn in your regular e-mail account with the information you requested.

Common e-mail notifications include:

- Connection invitations received
- Copies of messages sent to you within LinkedIn
- Daily summaries
- Activity summaries from your Groups (Groups are discussed in detail in Lesson 7)

On the LinkedIn site, you can receive Updates in your LinkedIn Inbox or see them on your LinkedIn Homepage. However, if you do not check your LinkedIn Homepage or Inbox on a regular basis, receiving e-mail notifications sent to your regular e-mail address can be useful.

You can configure and adjust the types and timing of e-mail notifications you receive under "E-mail Preferences" in your LinkedIn Settings (discussed in more detail in Lesson 10). We recommend receiving notifications in an HTML format so that you can click on links in the messages to go to the invitation, Profile, or other item on LinkedIn's Web site.

If you want Updates to come to you without having to go to your Homepage or clutter your e-mail inbox with more e-mail, subscribing to a personalized RSS feed is a great option. You can subscribe to an RSS feed through a choice in the Account options in your LinkedIn Settings (see Figure 9.3).

Figure 9.3: RSS Subscription Option

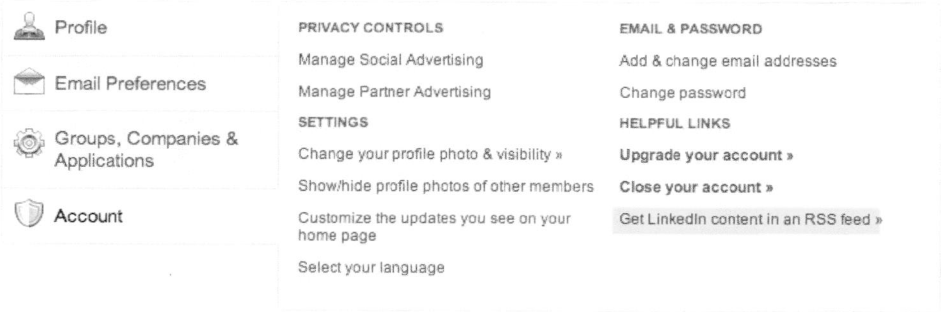

If you use Google Reader as your RSS reader, simply follow the directions to add the RSS feed to your list of feed subscriptions. After that, you will be able to view updates in Google Reader. We suggest putting that feed into a separate folder in Google Reader rather than mixing it in among the other feeds you read.

Method 3: Mobile Apps

As we become increasingly mobile and rely on our smartphones and tablet devices, we receive more information than ever on these devices.

Mobile apps have become important for many people and often become the primary way that people use online services.

LinkedIn has a very good mobile app, and it is free. The app is available for iOS, Android, and BlackBerry devices, either through the applicable app store or as a download from LinkedIn (**http://www.linkedin .com/static?key=mobile**). You can also use the slimmed-down mobile version of LinkedIn on your mobile phone if you do not have the app installed (**http://m.linkedin.com** or **http://touch.www.linkedin.com**).

LinkedIn introduced a major redesign of its mobile app in late 2011, giving it a simple, uncluttered design and an emphasis on the main activities you will want to perform on LinkedIn (see Figure 9.4).

Figure 9.4: LinkedIn Mobile Apps

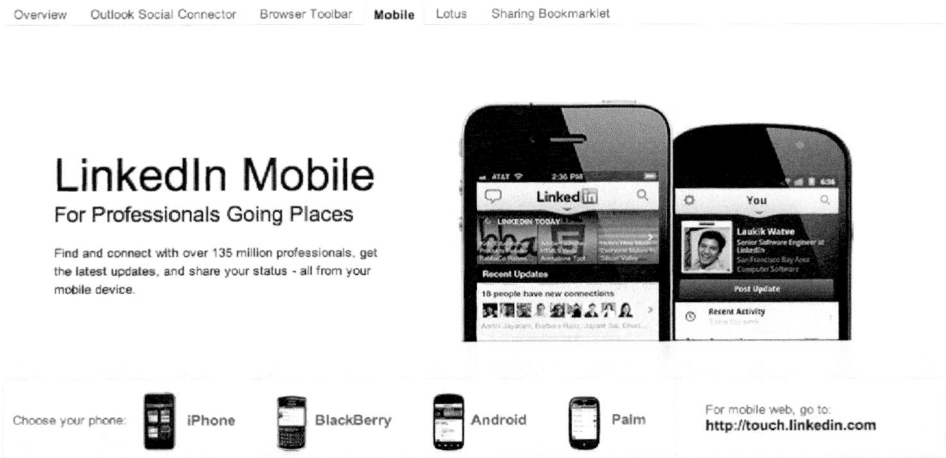

Let us take a quick look at the iPhone App to give you an idea about what to expect. The app's icon on your iPhone will have a number indicating that you have unread messages in your inbox so that you can tell when there are waiting messages or invitations before you even open the app. When you open the app, you will see four boxes: Updates, Inbox, You, and Groups & More (see Figure 9.5). At the top of the screens are icons that let you conduct searches and post your own updates. Simply tap your finger on the box you want to see.

Figure 9.5: LinkedIn iPhone/iPad App

The Updates section gives you quick access to the updates that you would see on the Homepage and lets you see the activity in your network. It is definitely a useful, well-conceived, and well-designed app that could easily become the primary way you interact with LinkedIn.

Benefits of Network Monitoring

LinkedIn tools work automatically and conveniently because they bring you the information provided from Updates supplied by those in your network. Think for a moment about how you use your standard contacts in Outlook or elsewhere. You might hear a contact has changed jobs. Because you have to make the change to his or her contact information in Outlook manually, it is possible that months go by before you update the contact's information with the new data. With LinkedIn, however, you automatically receive a notice of the change in real time because the contact changed his or her LinkedIn Profile. You will also know to call the contact and congratulate him or her or ask how the new job is going the next time you see the contact in person.

Monitoring your network should be a regular, ongoing process. Putting your eyes and ears on your network has never been easier than it is with LinkedIn. In many ways, LinkedIn does all the work for you and lets you know what is happening in your network. With that, you can take appropriate steps to respond to Updates, tend to your network, and create value in and from your network.

Let us go to our final Lesson, where we help you optimize LinkedIn settings to protect your privacy and customize your LinkedIn experience.

Optimizing Your Settings

It is impossible to overestimate the importance of choosing appropriate privacy and other settings in social media. You must understand your settings options and their implications. Accepting default settings in social media tools simply means that you are choosing what is best for the company offering the tool, not what is best for you.

Although historically LinkedIn has had a better track record than Facebook and other social media tools, lawyers (and others) should be wary of default settings. The good news is that LinkedIn offers a large number of choices for personalizing your experience, choosing appropriate settings, and revealing and managing your information in the way that makes the most sense for you. LinkedIn also groups the controls in one convenient location.

Work your way through all the settings step by step, either when you create your account or the next time you log into your account. It will take only a few minutes. Then plan to revisit your settings once or twice a year, if you learn that LinkedIn has made changes to privacy settings, or if you notice that you are receiving too many e-mails or have other annoyances. Often what might be bothering you about LinkedIn can be remedied with a quick change to your settings.

To get started, simply click on the "Settings" link available under your name at the top of every page (see Figure 10.1).

Figure 10.1: Settings Submenu

In one handy location, LinkedIn gives you many options to tailor your privacy controls; settings for Groups, Companies and Applications; and other account options (see Figure 10.2).

Figure 10.2: Settings Page

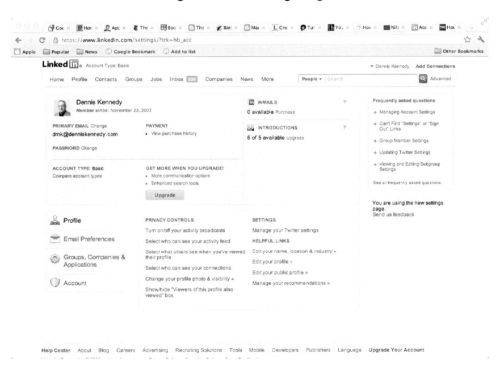

Privacy-Related Settings

Lawyers are and should be concerned with privacy-related settings. Under your Profile settings (see Figure 10.2), you will see six privacy settings you can adjust:

- **Activity Broadcasts.** Control whether people can see when you change your Profile, follow Companies, or make Recommendations. You might change this if you are looking for a job and do not want your employer to discover that.
- **Activity Feed.** Limit who can see your activities and Updates (discussed in Lesson 8) to yourself, your Connections, or your Network, or make them visible to everyone.
- **Profile Views.** Control what information is shown if you view other users' Profiles. You can choose your name and headline, an anonymous generic description ("Someone at Your Firm") or remain totally anonymous.
- **Show or Hide Your Connections.** Although it might be tempting for some lawyers to make their Connections visible only to themselves: (1) hiding Connections defeats a primary purpose of networking through LinkedIn; and (2) many LinkedIn users simply will not add you as a Connection if you hide your Connections. LinkedIn users, however, will always be able to see shared Connections.
- **Profile Photos.** Make your photo visible to your Connections, your network, or everyone.
- **Show/Hide "Viewers of this Profile Also Viewed" Information.** Turn this feature on or off.

There are also two more privacy settings under your Account Settings: managing social advertising and partner advertising you might receive through LinkedIn. Most lawyers will want to make sure that the box under the social advertising setting "LinkedIn may use my name, photo in social advertising" is not checked. You will also want to read LinkedIn's privacy policy.

Profile Settings

We discussed Profiles in detail in Lessons 2 and 3, but you can also configure and change your Profile under the Profile options on the Settings page. You can easily edit your Profile, add a picture, or control who sees your picture and even claim a "Vanity LinkedIn URL" for your Profile page (**http://www.linkedin.com/YOURNAME/**).

The other important thing you can do under Profile settings is to manage Recommendations under the "Manage Your Recommendations" option. We will discuss legal ethics issues in the Advanced Topics section of this book, but here you can show, hide, or request revisions to recommendations. Because of the interplay of LinkedIn Recommendations and ethical rules involving endorsements, these are important settings for lawyers to understand and use.

Account Settings

You can add, remove, or change an e-mail address associated with your account. This setting will be important if you change jobs (see Figure 10.3).

Figure 10.3: Account Settings Options

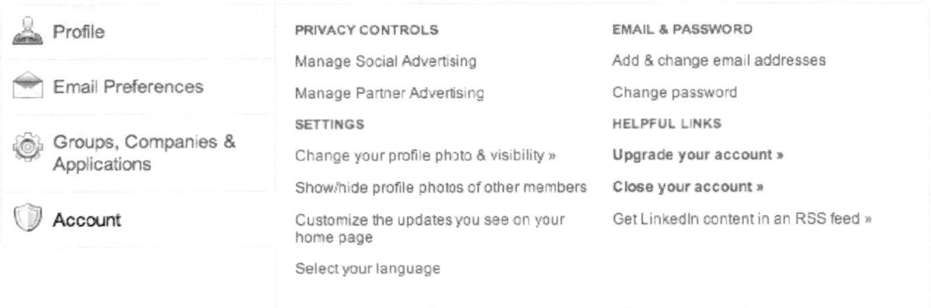

Profile	PRIVACY CONTROLS	EMAIL & PASSWORD
	Manage Social Advertising	Add & change email addresses
Email Preferences	Manage Partner Advertising	Change password
	SETTINGS	HELPFUL LINKS
Groups, Companies & Applications	Change your profile photo & visibility »	Upgrade your account »
	Show/hide profile photos of other members	Close your account »
Account	Customize the updates you see on your home page	Get LinkedIn content in an RSS feed »
	Select your language	

You can also change passwords from this screen. Here are two key pointers about passwords: (1) do not use the same password for LinkedIn that you use for any other accounts; (2) always use strong passwords—combinations of eight or more characters including upper- and lower-case letters, numbers, and special characters.

If you have had a LinkedIn account for awhile, we recommend that you change your password right now. Why? Because you need to be smart about passwords, and it is important to change passwords from time to time. If someone hacks your LinkedIn account, they can damage your professional presence in view of your most important contacts.

E-mail Preferences

The "E-mail Preferences" give you a good number of choices for customizing the types and volume of e-mail you receive from LinkedIn (see Figure 10.4).

Figure 10.4: E-mail Preferences Options

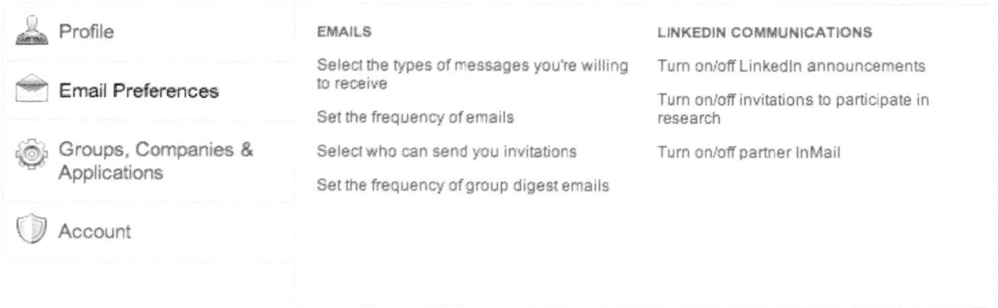

Profile	EMAILS	LINKEDIN COMMUNICATIONS
	Select the types of messages you're willing to receive	Turn on/off LinkedIn announcements
Email Preferences	Set the frequency of emails	Turn on/off invitations to participate in research
Groups, Companies & Applications	Select who can send you invitations	Turn on/off partner InMail
	Set the frequency of group digest emails	
Account		

Take a look at the options and choose what makes sense for you. Then watch the volume of e-mail you get and make adjustments accordingly. If you find that you receive too many random invitations or invitations that seem like spam, you have the option to limit who can send you unsolicited invitations.

Groups, Companies, and Applications Settings

We discuss Groups, Companies, and Applications in other sections of this book, but LinkedIn gives you controls over those features as well, all conveniently located on the Settings page.

Your LinkedIn experience is something that you must plan to pay attention to on a regular basis. In no area is that more true than in the area of account settings. LinkedIn gives you a lot of control, and you should make sure to take advantage of that to protect your privacy and enhance your experience.

Next, we wrap up the Lessons section and give you three simple action steps any reader can take right now to improve the value of LinkedIn.

Developing a Simple LinkedIn Strategy and Three Action Steps

Congratulations! You have learned the basics about the three essential building blocks of LinkedIn that you must master: Profiles, Connections, and Participation. You should also be seeing how LinkedIn both tracks and enhances the networking you do in the real world. Now it is time to put together a basic strategy for using LinkedIn and turn it into a great tool that works for you and your practice with three simple action steps.

1. Profile

The easiest place to begin is with your Profile. If you have not already created your basic, bare-bones LinkedIn Profile, do that first. If you have a Profile already, now is the time to begin putting some meat on those bones and fleshing it out to give a more complete picture of who you are and what you do for your clients.

Make sure your Profile includes:

- Photo
- Current and past positions
- Education
- Summary including what you do for clients in language they use and understand
- Any necessary disclaimers

We suggest working on your Profile weekly (thirty minutes per week should do it) until you reach "100% completeness" and then using the "Improve your Profile" button to continue to make enhancements. Revisit your Profile periodically to update it and add content.

Your Profile Action Step. Reread and rewrite your Profile summary so that it has an external focus that tells readers exactly what you want them to know about you so that they will want to connect with you.

Connections

Upload your contacts into LinkedIn and begin sending out invitations. Work first with those individuals who are already on LinkedIn (remember that once your contacts are uploaded, LinkedIn will show you who is a member by placing the "in" logo next to their name).

Search for potential Connections by seeking out classmates, former colleagues, and members of Groups to which you belong who may not be included in your current contact database.

Add Connections gradually over time. Remember to personalize the invitations to make them more effective.

Your Connections Action Step. Try one (or more) of the three power connecting techniques in Lesson 4 and try to set and reach a reasonable goal for your total number of Connections.

Participation

You will get the most out of LinkedIn if you actively participate and use it to create relationships. You have learned how to do that by joining and actively engaging with Groups, posting Updates (both individual and firm-wide), monitoring your Connections, and answering questions.

Begin by joining three Groups. Review Group activity weekly for interesting discussions and opportunities to participate. Consider posting regular Updates. Take your LinkedIn relationships offline: send e-mails, meet for coffee or lunch, or call your Connections on the telephone. Make an effort to find out which of your LinkedIn Connections will be attending seminars or conferences you attend and plan to meet them in person by checking their updates or exploring the Events features of LinkedIn.

Your Participation Action Step. Try to post at least one Update per week for a month.

Building relationships takes time, whether in person or online. Use LinkedIn to identify and gain information about people you have just met or will be meeting, and keep using it to strengthen relationships and expand your network.

Participation on LinkedIn can help you identify and learn about potential clients, strategic alliances, and referral sources, and they can be a good way to get the word out about what you are doing, build relationships, and establish your expertise. As the "professional social network," LinkedIn is a great entry point into social media for lawyers and one with real-world benefits.

Ethical Considerations

In addition to being mindful of good social networking practices in general, lawyers also must be keenly aware of the ethical rules that govern lawyers' activities within their jurisdiction. Some of those ethical rules impact lawyers' participation on LinkedIn. We encourage all lawyers to regularly review the ethical rules and recent ethics opinions in their jurisdictions, especially because many of those rules have not yet caught up with new technologies or are being actively revised as this book was written to include specific references to social media, including LinkedIn. As of press time, there have been only a few ethical opinions that address LinkedIn specifically (in Florida and South Carolina), but there are opinions in some jurisdictions about electronic communications and other social media outlets that may be instructive.

We will cover some of the main ethical issues that might arise with lawyers' use of LinkedIn in this section, referring to the ABA Model Rules, but many states have different (and more strict) rules, so it is important that you become familiar with your own state's rules. Given the professional use of LinkedIn and the focus on Profiles and providing useful information, we expect that LinkedIn will be viewed as more analogous to standard law firm Web sites rather than television ads or other controversial areas. And, of course, we disclaim that we are giving any legal advice in this section. Rules and opinions do change, developments occur, and you must draw your own conclusions about the rules that apply to you. In summary:

- Regulation of social media, including LinkedIn, is an evolving topic; therefore, you must keep abreast of developments (because of the high level of LinkedIn usage by lawyers, you are likely to see plenty of coverage of any developments impacting LinkedIn usage)
- Know and understand the opinions and approaches of the applicable jurisdictions for you and your practice
- Follow the core principle of avoiding the dissemination of misleading information
- Use appropriate and applicable disclaimers required in your jurisdiction(s)
- Have a solid understanding of the advertising and solicitation rules, including those about specialties and endorsements
- Implement a social media policy or add coverage of social media to existing firm policies

False or Misleading Information

As a general rule, lawyers are prohibited from making false or misleading statements about themselves or their services. This rule is contained in ABA Model Rule 7.1.

To avoid being misleading, a lawyer or law firm must keep any online presence, including a LinkedIn Profile, up to date and ensure that disclaimers prevent creating unjustified expectations in the mind of the Web site visitor (see *Disclaimers*, below).

For lawyers who have blogs or who post articles on their LinkedIn Profiles, it may be wise to date the post or article and include a notice that the legal information was accurate as of the date of the writing, but that the law changes frequently, and that readers should not rely on the online information, but should consult a lawyer who can discuss their specific factual situation. Outdated or inaccurate information should be removed.

Disclaimers

ABA Model Rule 7.3(c) requires that every electronic communication from a lawyer soliciting professional employment from a prospective client known to be in need of legal services in a particular matter include the words "Advertising Material," unless it falls under one of the exceptions listed in Rule 7.3. Many jurisdictions share this requirement.

You can add a disclaimer to your LinkedIn Profile in your Contact Settings that will appear on the section of your Profile that reads, "Contact [your name] for." To add the disclaimer, click on "Change Contact Preferences" on the Edit Profile screen. You will see a box entitled, "What advice would you give to users considering contacting you?" Add your required disclaimers into this box, along with any instructions for those who want to contact you (you might refer them to your Web site or advise them to call your office rather than contact you through LinkedIn).

Whether your jurisdiction requires it or not, it is wise to include some kind of disclaimer on your LinkedIn Profile indicating that visiting your Profile, viewing presentations or other content, or contacting you through LinkedIn does not establish a lawyer-client relationship, and that this contact might not be confidential. Make sure your disclaimers are clear and easy to understand.

Confidentiality

Confidentiality of client communications is one of the cornerstones of legal practice. ABA Model Rule 1.6 governs confidentiality of information and notes that a lawyer shall not reveal information relating to the representation of a client unless the client gives informed consent. Posting about ongoing client matters in Updates or within Groups—even without mentioning a client by name—can be problematic. In fact, posting about "live" cases and matters might be the hottest area in legal ethics today.

Communications through LinkedIn can also raise confidentiality issues, and lawyers should take care to ensure that the confidentiality of communications with prospective clients is preserved when responding to questions on LinkedIn. Lawyers should provide only general responses and should caution those asking questions on LinkedIn, whether in Answers or Groups or even through InMail, that confidentiality cannot be expected.

Connecting to current clients may also raise some confidentiality issues, particularly for clients with sensitive legal matters such as bankruptcy or divorce, although the risk may be somewhat diminished because the client must consent to the Connection. In addition, it is unclear whether anyone looking at your LinkedIn Profile or your Connections would know that the individual was a client, as opposed to a neighbor, friend, colleague, co-worker, etc., but consider confidentiality issues when requesting or accepting client invitations.

Advertising

Most jurisdictions have special rules governing lawyer advertising. Is your LinkedIn Profile considered "advertising"? In many jurisdictions, the answer is "yes."

The ABA issued an ethics opinion, ABA Formal Opinion 10-457 on Lawyer Websites, in August of 2010, which provides that, if online activities promote a law practice, they are considered lawyer advertising. That means that if your LinkedIn Profile (or Company Page) promotes you as a lawyer, it is considered an advertisement and must comply with the advertising rules. Is a LinkedIn Profile simply informational or is it promotional? Reasonable minds can reach different conclusions. However, it is realistic to expect that bar regulators will err on the side of finding a LinkedIn Profile to be advertising, based on what regulators have done in other Internet settings.

ABA Model Rule 7.2 covers advertising. Rule 7.2(c) requires any communication considered advertising to include the name and office address of at least one lawyer or law firm responsible for its content. If your jurisdiction's rule is similar, be sure that your firm's office address appears somewhere in your LinkedIn Profile.

Some states require prior review of advertisements or solicitations (for more on solicitations, see below), giving rise to questions about whether your LinkedIn Profile could be posted or substantially updated, or whether embedded videos or presentations could be posted, without prior review. For example, under Texas rule 7.07, law firm advertising must be submitted to the Advertising Review Committee. It has been determined that law firm or individual lawyer videos uploaded to sites like YouTube and Facebook must be submitted for review. It is unclear whether regular social networking updates must also be submitted. Texas seems to have clarified that certain social media sites, such as LinkedIn, do not, but you must, of course, confirm that for yourself and your jurisdiction.

Solicitation

Many states have special rules concerning solicitation, separate and apart from the general rules governing lawyer advertising. Generally, solicitation is distinguished from advertising because it involves direct contact with a specific person (or group of people) for the purpose of getting the lawyer hired, rather than a general advertisement sent or available to the general public. Individual requests to connect or direct messages through InMail might be considered solicitations in some circumstances.

In 2010, the Philadelphia Bar Association issued an opinion (Philadelphia Bar Assn. Profl. Guidance Comm., Op. 2010-6) that its Rule 7.3 does *not* bar lawyers from using social media for solicitation where the prospective client has the ability to ignore the soliciting lawyer. Given that those receiving invitations to connect on LinkedIn can ignore the request and simply not respond, this opinion might be read to permit lawyers to solicit using LinkedIn.

ABA Model Rule 7.3 governs direct contact with prospective clients. Subsection (a) prohibits "real-time electronic contact [to] solicit professional employment from a prospective client when a significant motive for the lawyer's doing so is the lawyer's pecuniary gain," with specific exceptions. Subsection (c) requires any such communication to include a disclaimer (see *Disclaimers* above).

Specialization and "Expert" Status

Although lawyers are permitted to communicate the areas of law in which they practice, many jurisdictions prohibit lawyers from proclaiming that they are "specialists" or "experts" in any particular field, absent special certification by an approved, accredited authority. ABA Model Rule 7.4 also requires that the name of the accrediting organization be clearly identified. This might make filling in "Specialties" on your LinkedIn Profile problematic if you are not certified in a particular specialty. Some lawyers have addressed this prohibition by putting a disclaimer in the "Summary" portion of their Profile, noting that the designated "specialties" are their practice areas. If you are concerned, simply fill in your Summary and leave Specialties blank.

The issue of specialization and "expert" status also arises with LinkedIn Answers. When the questioner rates the answers provided, LinkedIn awards "expert" points and will designate you as an "expert" once you have reached a certain threshold number of points. Although LinkedIn makes the designation, not the lawyer, the designation will appear with the lawyer's name and picture, and many jurisdictions require lawyers to ensure that what others say about them does not violate ethical rules. To avoid this problem, lawyers can answer questions within LinkedIn Groups, where there is no such expert designation.

Inadvertent Lawyer-Client Relationship and Unauthorized Practice of Law

Answering questions and participating on social networking sites means that your message is disseminated to those outside the jurisdiction in which you practice. As such, you must be mindful of ABA Model Rule 5.5, which prohibits the unauthorized practice of law or practice outside of a jurisdiction in which you are admitted to practice, subject to certain exceptions.

You should also use caution when answering questions on LinkedIn, just as you would on sites such as Avvo, to be sure that you are not creating an inadvertent lawyer-client relationship or offering legal advice. ABA Formal Opinion 10-457 cites several cases from a variety of states noting that because lawyers cannot screen for conflicts of interest when answering questions posted on the Internet, lawyers should refrain from answering specific legal questions unless the advice given is not fact-specific. However, it should be noted that many jurisdictions do permit lawyers to answer hypothetical questions. It is also important to remember that whether a lawyer-client relationship is created has historically been determined from the client's perspective.

In addition, in determining whether a lawyer-client relationship has been established or a lawyer has violated the prohibition against unauthorized practice of law, the rules and opinions place a great deal of importance on who controls the flow of information and whether that information is provided unilaterally or is part of a bilateral discussion, as well as the subsequent actions of the lawyer or firm once the communication is received (see ABA Formal Opinion 10-457 and ABA Model Rule 1.18).

Recommendations

Some jurisdictions prohibit testimonials or Recommendations entirely, whereas others allow them from former, but not current, clients. Still others permit all testimonials. Most jurisdictions require some kind of disclaimer to accompany these testimonials. If this is the case in your jurisdiction, you might need to provide those who recommend you on LinkedIn with disclaimer language to place at the bottom of their Recommendation. To make these issues even more complicated, some states differentiate between "testimonials" and "endorsements."

As we explained above, lawyers are responsible not only for what they publish on the Web about themselves, but also for what others publish about them. Although Recommendations can be great for your practice, you must diligently review them to ensure that your clients are not using prohibited words that you would be prevented from using by your jurisdiction's ethical rules. The general standard is that you can make claims that can be objectively proven. Phrases like "best tax lawyer in America" or "most awesome real estate lawyer ever" would not meet the objectively provable standard. You must also be sure that the Recommendation cannot be considered false or misleading. Remember that you can approve and manage the Recommendations you receive before they are posted.

According to ABA Model Rule 7.2(b), lawyers are prohibited from giving anything of value to a person for recommending the lawyer's services. How does that impact your LinkedIn participation? Do not offer reciprocal Recommendations (i.e., "if you recommend me, I will recommend you.").

General Tips

The best rule of thumb when considering what you can and cannot do on LinkedIn (or any other social networking site) is not to say anything that you would not be comfortable saying or doing in a room full of people or publishing on the front page of the *Wall Street Journal*. A corollary would be to be cautious about saying anything about the details of a current case or matter.

Make sure you have a social media policy for your law firm that clearly spells out the firm's guidelines for use of social media by everyone in the office.

Watch out for specialized issues that arise out of social media usage. For example, the use of social media by and with judges has already raised a number of questions. Become familiar with the ethical rules in your jurisdiction about friending on Facebook or connecting with judges on LinkedIn and other social media and using social media as an investigative tool in for potential jurors, witnesses, and opposing parties.

Final Thoughts

In many ways, behavior on LinkedIn and social media is identical, at least conceptually, to behavior in the physical world, and the same ethical principles will apply. When considering activities on LinkedIn, think about the ethical implications of comparable real-world activities. If you take that approach, stay mindful of the basic principle of avoiding misrepresentation, and stay aware of your state's specific rules or guidelines, you should be in good shape on the ethical front. However, social media is constantly evolving, and we expect ethical regulations will continue to evolve as regulators better understand social media tools. As in the real world, you must keep abreast of current developments.

Using LinkedIn in the Hiring Process

LinkedIn has been used as a job-seeking tool since its inception. People in the recruiting business say that the LinkedIn Profile has already replaced the traditional paper resume, especially in certain fields. LinkedIn even has a handy tool for turning your Profile into a traditional resume. In fact, for many years, LinkedIn users have associated a flurry of Profile updates and additions to Connections by one of their Connections as a sign that the person is looking for a new job.

For job seekers, LinkedIn facilitates job searches through the information and tools collected under the "Jobs" menu tab you can find at the top of the Homepage. In addition to finding openings, you might use your Connections and the search tools to find people to talk to as potential employers or research the interviewers to whom you will be talking.

In this section, we focus on the other side of the equation: how can you use LinkedIn to assist you when hiring new people? If you have interviewed candidates recently, you might have already noticed the impact of LinkedIn. Well-prepared candidates seem to know more about your background than ever before. They might mention names of people that you know and that they know. They might even say that they talked to a friend of yours who told them that it would be great to work with you. Although this can sometimes seem a little unsettling, it also leaves a favorable impression about the preparedness of the candidate. It also shows that they know how to use LinkedIn.

Simply flip things around and you will see that you can do the same things when preparing to interview a candidate. The candidate's LinkedIn Profile might give you much more detailed information than a traditional one-page resume. The Profile might be more informal and plainly written than a formal resume. If the candidate has Recommendations on his or her Profile, you might get a better picture of the candidate's capabilities or even learn that you know one of the recommenders.

Best of all, you can check out what shared Connections you might have with a candidate so that you can talk about those relationships in the interview or even informally "vet" the candidate with a trusted Connection.

And that is just the beginning. Here are six quick ways that you can use LinkedIn during your hiring process. Once you use LinkedIn for these purposes, you will probably find other great ideas as well.

1) Post an update indicating that you have a job opening and ask your Connections to put the word out to people who might be a good fit for your firm or organization.

2) Explore the Company Page of the firm for which a candidate works to get a better picture of what his or her work experience might really be and learn about the candidate's colleagues and supervisors.

3) View how the candidate has used the "Skills" component of LinkedIn (see Lesson 3 on improving your Profile) and what Skills the candidate has highlighted, and then compare them to what the candidate highlights in the interview (and what skills the job requires).

4) Incorporate mentions of shared Connections into your interviews.

5) Monitor your Network Updates for ideas about who might be interested in joining your organization. Observe changes in firms or note a Connection who might be looking for a new job. You might notice that someone you thought was content in his or her current

position is actually looking for a job or might be receptive to your inquiry because others are leaving his or her firm.

6) Read the Updates and other information the candidate makes public and the Groups he or she has joined to gauge areas of interest.

Much as LinkedIn changed the resume process, it has the potential to change the hiring and interviewing process as well. There are great potential benefits, but not surprisingly, LinkedIn raises some new hiring etiquette issues. Here is one interesting question: should you accept an invitation to connect from a candidate during the interview process or extend your invitation to connect during the interview process? Watch as LinkedIn becomes part of the hiring process and observe ways that you can use LinkedIn to help you hire the best people.

LinkedIn Apps

LinkedIn offers a relatively limited number of useful apps that can enhance your LinkedIn experience. What LinkedIn lacks in quantity of apps today is more than made up for by the quality and utility of these apps. LinkedIn apps fall into two categories: the LinkedIn mobile app for smartphones (discussed in Lesson 9) and apps that run inside LinkedIn (we will refer to them as "LinkedIn Apps"). We highly recommend that you install and use the mobile LinkedIn app. We also recommend that you consider using some of the LinkedIn Apps.

General LinkedIn Apps

There currently are a total of eighteen general LinkedIn Apps, a far more manageable number than the thousands of Facebook apps. We expect the number of LinkedIn Apps will continue to grow. LinkedIn also has a great Frequently Asked Questions page that answers the questions you might have about getting started with LinkedIn Apps (**https://help.linkedin.com/app/answers/detail/a_id/1160**).

The LinkedIn Apps, as a general matter, allow you to pull information from other sources to enhance your Profile and LinkedIn presence and provide additional value to your network. The current list includes:

- **Creative Portfolio Display**—Showcase your creative work, including presentations or other published material.
- **Box.Net Files**—Manage and share files online for collaboration purposes.

- **Google Presentations**—Upload presentations in Google Presentations and have them embedded in your Profile.
- **SlideShare Presentations**—Upload and show your presentations in SlideShare and view presentations from your Connections.
- **MyTravel**—From Tripit, share trip information and see who in your network will be traveling to the same city as you will be.
- **Reading List by Amazon**—Share the books you and those in your network are reading.
- **E-Bookshelf**—From FT Press, obtain and read business-related content.
- **Huddle Workspaces**—Create private, secure online workspaces for collaboration with selected Connections.
- **Rofo Real Estate Pro**—Access local real estate and office listings.
- **GitHub**—For software developers, showcase GitHub projects.
- **Events**—Find professional events and learn which of your Connections are attending them. Alternatively, post your own events and invite others to attend.
- **Projects and Teamspaces**—Share and track projects, tasks, and documents with selected Connections.
- **Polls**—Conduct surveys and get information from your network.
- **WordPress**—Sync WordPress blog posts with your Profile.
- **Blog Link**—Connect your blog to LinkedIn.
- **Tweets**—Manage a Twitter account.
- **Lawyer Ratings**—Show your Martindale-Hubbell ratings.
- **Legal Updates**—From JD Supra, get legal news and upload your own legal articles and materials for your network.

Is LinkedIn really a tool for lawyers? Note that the last two of the eighteen LinkedIn Apps are specifically directed toward lawyers.

In general, the LinkedIn Apps work in both your Profile and your Homepage. On your Homepage, they help you monitor what is happening in your network. On your Profile, they allow you to automatically incorporate materials you post on your blog, Twitter, or SlideShare, for example. As a result, your LinkedIn Profile can become a "hub" or "mini-portal" to the rest of your Internet presence.

If you already have a blog or use Twitter, SlideShare, or JD Supra, it makes great sense to try out some of the LinkedIn Apps. Currently, LinkedIn puts a limit of twelve LinkedIn Apps on your Profile and fifteen LinkedIn Apps on your Homepage.

Company Buzz

Company Buzz is another app that lawyers might find especially useful. Company Buzz is a tool that helps you monitor what people are saying about your firm or organization or about a client or competitor. You can watch to see when people tweet about your firm or certain keywords. It also helps you respond quickly to questions or comments made about your firm or organization. There are even tools to graph frequency of mentions and other analytics.

Apps are an easy and free way to enhance your LinkedIn experience and effectiveness. We recommend that you try at least a few of them.

Company Pages

In addition to your individual Profile, you (or a designated individual, such as a marketing director in a large law firm) can create a Company Page for your law firm. All employees of your firm who have a Profile on LinkedIn will automatically be attached to your Company Page, giving those individual Profiles additional exposure. Having a page for your firm on LinkedIn allows you to provide firm-wide information, not specific to any individual. You can expand your client base and demonstrate your firm's expertise even more through the use of Company Pages and Company Updates.

Creating Your Company Page
When creating your Company Page, you will go through a similar process to creating your individual Profile, providing a description of your firm and then designating "Specialties" (note that ethical issues involving specialties are discussed in the Advanced Topics section of this book). Enable your Company Page for Updates and set permissions for those who are able to post on the Company Page on behalf of your firm.

Company Updates
On your Company Page, post firm-wide Updates, events, and firm news manually on a regular basis. Once people find your Company Page, they can "follow" your firm's News or Updates, or you can invite them to follow your firm on LinkedIn, much the same as you would advertise your firm's Facebook page and ask others to "like" your page.

Updates are seen on followers' Homepages, where they can share, like, or comment on your Updates. Using the same principles that we discussed in Lesson 8 for individual Updates, LinkedIn provides valuable links and news in your firm's Company Updates to help get your message out. It can be a great way to point people to items on your Web site or firm newsletter. Company Updates can be up to 500 characters long, which is plenty of room to provide summary information, links, and details about upcoming events.

Products and Services

The "Products and Services" area of Company Pages provides a place to describe your practice areas and services in more detail and provides individual links directly to specific pages on your Web site for more information. Alternatively, if you have created videos about your practice or about what you do for clients, you can link to those videos directly from the Products and Services tab. You can also add logos and images to make your descriptions more interesting.

For each service, you can identify a Company contact, which will allow you to let the individual practice group leader within your firm be contacted. A key feature not to be overlooked by lawyers is that you can even add a disclaimer in a designated section if you determine that you need one (see discussion of disclaimers in the Ethical Considerations section of this book).

Company Recommendations

There also is a Recommendations feature for Company Pages. It is connected to the Products and Services tab, and individuals can write Recommendations for each individual Product or Service, or you can request Recommendations for your Products and Services from those in your network. Sharing is also enabled for Products and Services, allowing others who see your Products and Services on LinkedIn to share that information with their network.

Tips for Company Pages

The key to making Company Pages work for you is to get creative about what you post and to actively engage on a consistent basis. You can benefit from increased interaction with other lawyers, strategic alliances, and referral sources and prospective clients.

As more and more businesses begin using Company Pages on LinkedIn, LinkedIn users will begin "following" these pages, just as they do on Facebook, Twitter, or other platforms. Given that LinkedIn is known as the professional network, however, those who follow your Updates on your Company Pages are likely to be those interested in your practice or your professional associations.

If your firm has a blog, you can connect it to your Company Page by filling in the blog's RSS feed. The title of each new blog post, along with the date it was posted, will be shown directly underneath the firm's employees on the Company Page.

There is also a News Module that allows you to display News about your Company; however, unless your firm is frequently in the media, you might want to check the "Don't show news about my company" box, given that LinkedIn pulls news about other businesses with similar names into your Company Page if there is no news about your firm.

Company Pages also include analytics features to track page views and visitors and compare with similar companies, and see who has been following and interacting with your Company Page (or your competitors' Company Pages).

Advanced Search Techniques

In Lesson 6, we covered the basics of using LinkedIn search and showed you some ways you can use search to find people or information. Now let us delve a bit deeper into LinkedIn's search capabilities.

Advanced People Search

Any time you can filter results using your own defined parameters, you are using LinkedIn's Advanced Search features. There is also an "Advanced" search button located next to the quick search box, but it relates only to People Search (see Figure A.1) or Answers. If you switch the quick search drop down from People to Companies or Groups, you will see that the link to Advanced search next to the search box disappears.

Figure A.1: Advanced Search Link

Clicking on Advanced search using People in the dropdown box brings you to the Advanced People Search screen. From this screen you can define parameters to filter your search and make it more specific (see Figure A.2). For example, you can search by:

- Name
- Location

Figure A.2: Advanced Search Page

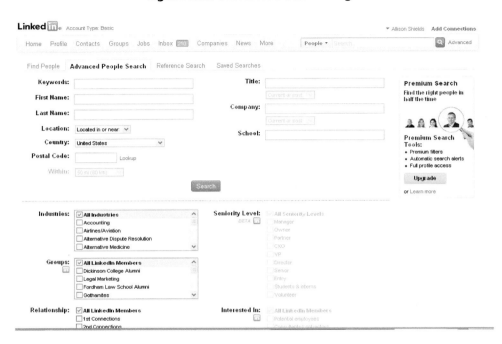

- Keyword
- Title
- Company
- School

You can also check boxes to specify an industry or refine further and limit your search to people who belong to a certain Group or filter by Relationship to see only first-level Connections, only second-level Connections, etc. There are additional filters available for those with a (paid) Premium Account.

Sort and Filter Search Results

You can also choose how results will be sorted when LinkedIn returns them to you. Sort by:

- Relevance
- Connections
- Keywords
- Relationship

Your results can be shown in either the Basic or Expanded view. In addition to name, headline, photo, location, and relationship, the Expanded view will show you the number of Connections and Recommendations the individual has on LinkedIn, as well as one current and one past position.

Saving Searches

If you perform the same kinds of searches over and over, you can save your search by clicking on "save" at the top of the search results. This will help you when you want to update your searches or search for new contacts within the same target market. You can save up to three searches with the free version of LinkedIn and have LinkedIn automatically run the search and e-mail you new results; if you want to save more than three searches, you must upgrade to a LinkedIn Premium account.

Searching Companies

Using LinkedIn Company Search might be an even better way to search than using People Search. You can search for Companies on the quick search bar (see Figure A.3) or go directly to Company Search under the "Companies" tab on the main LinkedIn navigation bar (see Figure A.4).

Figure A.3: Quick Search for Companies

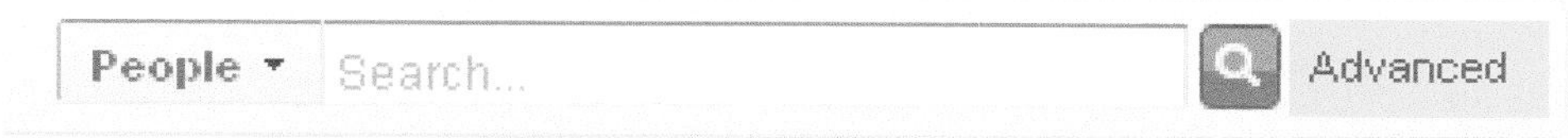

Figure A.4: Companies Search Submenu

Using this method will take you to the Companies Home page (see Figure A.5). Then, either enter your search terms in the box or click on the "Search Companies" tab (see Figure A.6).

Figure A.5: Companies Home Page

Figure A.6: Search Companies Tab

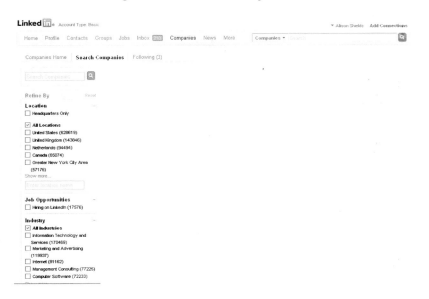

Define your search parameters in the left-hand column. You can refine your search by location, industry, or relationship (everyone on LinkedIn, only first-level Connections, etc.) LinkedIn also has premium filters that only LinkedIn Premium users can use, including years of experience, company size, Groups, and seniority level, among others.

Making Use of Company Page Information

The Profiles of the individuals who work for a company will be associated with the Company Page, making it easy to identify the appropriate contacts and how they might already be connected to your network. Click on "See all" to view the number of Connections you have in common (see Figure A.7). That is your way to get an introduction to the company. In addition to the shared Connections, you can also view the Groups you have in common with individuals at the company.

Figure A.7: See All Connections

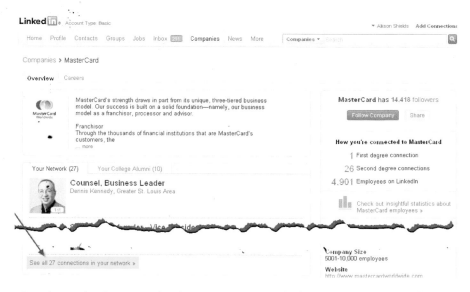

Look at the keywords the company and the individuals within that company use to describe their business. Are you using those keywords in your LinkedIn Profile to attract them? To what Groups do the individuals in the company belong? What Connections do you have to these individuals? Are any of them in your network?

When you find a company or business you are interested in, you can "follow" that company by clicking on the "Follow Company" button on the right sidebar. By doing so, you will receive every update that company shares on LinkedIn—new job postings, new hires, promotions, company news, etc. This will provide you with opportunities to reach out and connect with the company or individuals within the company. For example, if someone at a target company has been promoted, you may want to send them a congratulations card.

Searching Groups

On the main LinkedIn navigation bar, go to Groups and click on "Your Groups." Then click on any of the Groups to which you belong and navigate to the "Members" tab (see Figure A.8). Here you will

Figure A.8: Members Tab

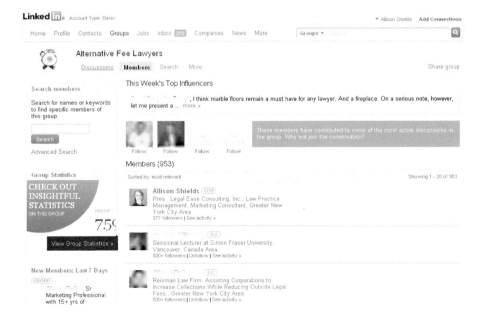

find a list of members. Scroll through the list to find people with whom to connect or use the Search Members box in the upper-left corner of the page to search by name or keyword. At the top of the Members page, LinkedIn will also show you who the "top influencers" are within the Group. These are people who have contributed to the most active discussions within the Group.

As you can see, LinkedIn's search features can provide you with almost unlimited opportunities to connect with people and provide you valuable information about your contacts—without ever having to leave LinkedIn.

Sixty LinkedIn Tips

1) LinkedIn's Help and Support materials (**http://learn.linkedin.com/**), including starter guides, are clearly written and useful. There is even a short user guide for lawyers (**http://learn.linkedin.com/attorneys/**).

2) Because LinkedIn has been around for a long time, many other people have had the same question you have. Check LinkedIn's frequently asked questions (**https://help.linkedin.com/app/topics**) to see if you can find the answer to your question.

3) Use a scheduling tool like HootSuite (**http://www.hootsuite.com**) to schedule LinkedIn Updates in advance and keep your Profile updated, even when you are on the go. If you participate in other social networks, including Facebook and Twitter, using HootSuite will allow you to post updates to multiple networks at once, all in one place.

4) Customize privacy and account settings on a regular basis.

5) Create a "vanity" URL for your Profile page.

6) Customize the Web site links on your Profile to give people reasons to visit your Web site, blog, or other sites.

7) Reorder your Profile according to what is most important to your audience.

8) Use the "Completeness Bar" and the "Improve Your Profile" button to create a robust LinkedIn Profile.

9) Make good use of your "Professional Headline" by giving it an external focus. Think of it as your LinkedIn "elevator speech."

10) Add Skills to your Profile. This relatively new feature might become helpful in fine-tuning who best fits your needs in hiring or other settings.

11) Have a plan for adding Connections (i.e., quality or quantity, local or global, inside your current organization or outside).

12) Do not blindly accept invitations—use them as an opportunity to create or advance relationships by sending the inviter a personal reply.

13) Always send personalized invitations so people remember you and are encouraged to accept your invitations.

14) Request recommendations (where appropriate).

15) Give recommendations (even if you cannot get them).

16) Become familiar with your jurisdiction's ethical rules affecting LinkedIn participation.

17) Take your online relationships offline—use LinkedIn to identify people with whom you can have lunch or attend a seminar or event.

18) When traveling, search your Connections to see which of your Connections live where you will be visiting and try to get together while in town.

19) Schedule regular weekly or monthly time for LinkedIn activities, including visiting your LinkedIn Homepage.

20) Regularly check LinkedIn for information about industries, clients, and potential clients and set up LinkedIn tools to bring you relevant information on a regular basis.

21) Create a Company Page for your law firm.

22) Use advanced search features to find and filter people.

23) Use Updates to send news and relevant links of value to your network.

24) Use self-promotion sparingly, self-deprecatingly, and subtly on LinkedIn. Always think about the actual value to others you bring

and think about how you would react to someone else doing the same thing.

25) Add any necessary legal disclaimers to your Profile page.

26) Add specifics about contacting you, lawyer-client relationships, and confidentiality in the Contact module on your Profile.

27) Add disclaimers to your Company Profile on the Products and Services pages.

28) Sync your blog and Twitter accounts to LinkedIn to allow for cross-posting and to get a bigger audience for information you post in other places.

29) Try some apps to your LinkedIn account: SlideShare, Google Presentation, etc.

30) Because LinkedIn allows you to connect with fellow Group members without requiring any additional information, such as their e-mail address, use Groups as a way to meet new people and make Connections.

31) "Follow" individuals of interest to you within a Group to receive their Updates. This is a great way to see what experts in your field are saying even though you are not connected to them.

32) Add links to your LinkedIn Profile on your Web site, blog, social media profiles, or other places you can be found on the Internet to let people get to your LinkedIn Profile no matter how they find you on the Internet.

33) Use the Recommendations approval controls to help avoid potential "endorsement" ethical issues.

34) The LinkedIn mobile app is excellent. And free. Download and install it.

35) Install the CardMunch card scanner app to help with handling business cards, especially at conferences.

36) Although you can start with a good personal photograph, invest in some good professional photographs to use on LinkedIn.

37) Facebook is the place for personal photos, vacation photos, and photos with other people in them. Not LinkedIn.

38) Use both the graduating year and the "years attended" filters in the Alumni Connections to connect with friends you went to schools with but were not in your graduating class.

39) Decide what you want to do about connecting with colleagues at your present employer. Your approach can make a big difference when you want to look for a new job and can affect what you decide to emphasize in your Profile, Groups you join, Updates, and much more.

40) Consider your audience with everything you post to LinkedIn.

41) Both asking and answering questions in Answers can be beneficial for lawyers.

42) Use LinkedIn to obtain competitive intelligence about other lawyers, firms, or your clients' competitors.

43) Read about some of the scientific research on social networking analysis (SNA) and topics like "strong" and "weak" links and Dunbar's number (the number of active Connections that you can reasonably expect to manage).

44) Read the Profile summaries of your Connections and model your summary on the ones you like best.

45) Always review the Connections, especially the Shared Connections, of anyone who sends you an invitation before accepting that Connection.

46) LinkedIn alerts you when someone who invites you to connect has no other Connections. Although having no or only a minimal number of Connections might indicate a new user, it could be a sign of a possible spam contact.

47) Always keep the real-world analogies in mind when using LinkedIn. If you are circumspect in connecting with or giving per-

sonal information in the real world, you will probably be most comfortable taking a similar approach on LinkedIn.

48) Review your Profile as a third party (or have someone do that for you). Watch for details that undercut what you are trying to say (e.g., if you claim you are a SuperLawyer, but have no Recommendations and only a handful of Connections, none of whom look like clients, people will wonder whether the claim is true.

49) If after you refer a client to another lawyer, finish a successful project or have a successful result, someone wants to connect on LinkedIn, ask them to consider writing a Recommendation in your reply.

50) You will probably achieve better business results from LinkedIn by concentrating on potential referrers rather than potential clients.

51) If you give presentations, add your slides to SlideShare and make them available through LinkedIn.

52) If you contribute to JD Supra, use the JD Supra app to make your contributions available through LinkedIn.

53) Consider setting up a separate "business" Twitter account if you use Twitter to post business content, which can be automatically turned into LinkedIn Updates.

54) If you are looking for a new job, LinkedIn's features, especially Jobs, can be indispensable.

55) If you are speaking at a conference or other event, use the Events feature to help promote the event or invite others to attend.

56) The "Who's Viewed Your Profile" and "Viewers of those Profile also Viewed" features can be quite interesting and even entertaining.

57) Do not interview or hire a job candidate without checking out his or her LinkedIn Profile and presence.

58) Read the LinkedIn blog to keep up with new developments, get great tips, and learn to use LinkedIn better.

59) There may be no better resource than LinkedIn to help you reconnect with people who were important in your legal career but with whom you have lost contact.

60) LinkedIn is an evolving service. Watch for new features and be willing to try them out.

Resources

American Bar Association, "ABA 20/20 Commission Initial Draft Proposals on Lawyers' Use of Technology and Client Development" (June 29, 2011). http://www.americanbar.org/content/dam/aba/administrative/ethics_2020/20110629ethics202technologyclientdevelopmentinitialresolutionsandreport.authcheckdam.pdf.

American Bar Association, "ABA Formal Opinion 10-457, Lawyer Websites," (issued Aug. 2010). http://www.americanbar.org/content/dam/aba/migrated/cpr/pdfs/10_457.authcheckdam.pdf.

American Bar Association, ABA Model Rules of Professional Conduct, http://www.americanbar.org/groups/professional_responsibility/publications/model_rules_of_professional_conduct/model_rules_of_professional_conduct_table_of_contents.html.

Barabasi, Albert-Laszlo, *Linked: How Everything Is Connected to Everything Else and What It Means,* Plume, 2003.

Breitbarth, Wayne, *The Power Formula for LinkedIn Success: Kickstart Your Business, Brand, and Job Search,* Greenleaf Book Group LLC, 2011.

Bruce, Debra, "12 Social Media Ethics Issues for Lawyers," SoloPractice University, http://solopracticeuniversity.com/2010/03/11/a-dozen-social-media-ethics-issues-for-lawyers/.

Elefant, Carolyn and Nicole Black, *Social Media for Lawyers: The Next Frontier,* American Bar Association, 2010.

Golden, Michelle, *Social Media Strategies for Professionals and Their Firms: The Guide to Establishing Credibility and Accelerating Relationships,* Wiley Professional Advisory, 2010.

Griffiths, Lindsey, LinkedIn Tutorials, *Zen & The Art of Legal Networking Blog,* http://www.zenlegalnetworking.com/admin/mt-xsearch .cgi?blog_id=1157&search_key=keyword&search=Linkedin+tutorial &Search.x=0&Search.y=0.

Hughes, Bryn, "Think social media is a waste of time? Your competitors don't . . . http://blog.martindale.com/think-social-media-is-a-waste-of-time-your-competitors-don't.

Kennedy-Mighell Report Podcast, "The Land of LinkedIn," http://legal talknetwork.com/podcasts/kennedy-mighell-report/2011/02/the-land-of-linkedin/.

Koblentz, Evan, "Lexis Says Social Networking Lags at Large Firms," *Law Technology News* (Dec. 13, 2011). http://www.law.com/jsp/ lawtechnologynews/PubArticleLTN.jsp?id=1202535285157.

LinkedIn Learning Center, http://learn.linkedin.com/.

LinkedIn Blog, http://blog.linkedin.com/.

LinkedIn Help Center, https://help.linkedin.com/app/home.

Lynda.com, LinkedIn Essential Training Video, http://www.lynda.com/ LinkedIn-tutorials/essential-training/73285-2.html.

Mackay, Harvey, *Dig Your Well Before You're Thirsty: The Only Networking Book You'll Ever Need,* Currency Books, 1999.

Poje, Joshua, J.D., "Legal Ethics and Policy Considerations in E-Communications and Social Media," ABA Legal Technology Resource Center, http://www.iml.org/files/pages/4213/LegalEthicsSocial Media.pdf.

Shields, Allison C., "The Professionals' Social Network: LinkedIn." http://www.americanbar.org/publications/law_practice_magazine/ 2012/january_february/the-professionals-social-network-linkedin .html.

Shields, Allison C., "LinkedIn: Tools for Lawyers." **http://lawyerist .com/linkedin-tools-for-lawyers/.**

Shields, Allison C, Dennis Kennedy, and Michelle Golden, "LinkedIn for Lawyers: A Practical Guide to the No. 1 Social Media Tool" (Audio), **http://www.ali-aba.org/index.cfm?fuseaction=courses .course&course_code=RSTP03&contenttype=4.**

Index

ABA Formal Opinion 10-457 (lawyer websites), 88–89, 91
ABA Model Rules
  1.6 (confidentiality), 87–88
  5.5 (unauthorized practice of law), 91
  7.1 (false/misleading information), 87
  7.2 (advertising), 88–89
  7.2(b) (recommendations), 92
  7.3 (solicitation), 89–90
  7.3(c) (disclaimers), 87
  7.4 (specialization and "expert" status), 90
Accounts, LinkedIn
  choosing basic or premium, 9–10
  confirming, 7–9
  creating, 7–9
  settings, 78–79
Action steps
  for Connections, 82
  for Participation, 82–83
  for Profile, 81–82
Advanced Search features
  for companies, 109–111
  for people, 107–108
  saving searches, 109
  sorting and filtering results, 108–109
Advertising, ethics and, 88–89
Alumni feature, for Connections, 33–34
Answers
  about, 59
  getting started with, 59–61
  to questions, 61
  tips, 62
Applications settings, 80

Apps
  Company Buzz, 101
  general LinkedIn, 99–101
  mobile, monitoring via, 71–74
Asymmetrical approach, 26

Basic accounts, 9–10
Blog Link app, 100
Box.Net Files app, 99
Brand, managing personal, and Profile, 20–21
Business cards, as source of Connections, 41

CardMunch, 41
Colleagues feature, for Connections, 31–33
Companies
  searching, 109–111
  settings, 80
Company Buzz app, 101
Company Pages
  about, 103
  creating, 103
  "Products and Services" area of, 104
  Recommendations feature for, 104–105
  tips for, 105
  updates, 103–104
  using information on, 111–112
Completeness bar, 17–18
Confidentiality, ethics and, 87–88
Connections. *See also* LinkedIn; Participation; Profile(s)
  accepting invitations for, 40
  action steps, 82
  adding, 26–27

adding colleagues and former colleagues for, 31–33
Alumni feature for, 33–34
defined, 3
Groups as source of, 40
importing existing contacts for, 27–31
in-person meetings for, 41
invitations from individual's Profiles for, 37–39
as ongoing process, 41–42
"People You May Know" tool, 36–37
principles, 25–26
Contacts, 26
importing existing, for Connections, 27–31
Creative Photo Display app, 99

Disclaimers, ethics and, 87

E-Bookshelf app, 100
Educational information, in Profile, 16
E-mail
monitoring via, 70–71
preference settings, 79
Ethics
about, 85–86
advertising and, 88–89
confidentiality and, 87–88
disclaimers and, 87
"expert" status and, 90
false/misleading information and, 86
general tips for, 92–93
recommendations and, 91–92
solicitation and, 89–90
specialization and, 90
unauthorized practice of law, 91
Events app, 100
Experience, listing, 16
"Expert" status, ethics and, 90

False information, ethics and, 86
Filtering, search results, 108–109
Former colleagues, as source of Connections, 31–33

GitHub app, 100
Google+, "asymmetrical" approach of, 26
Google Presentations app, 100
Groups
about, 54
benefits of, 56–57
finding, to join, 54–55
searching, 112–113
settings, 80
as source of Connections, 40
starting your own, 57–58
tips for, 56

Headline, professional, 15
Hiring process, LinkedIn and, 95–97. *See also* Resumes, using Profile for
Homepage, 68–70
Huddle Workspaces app, 100

Information, false/misleading, ethics and, 86
InMail feature, 37
In-person meetings, for Connections, 41
Invitations
accepting, 40
sending, 37–39
iPhone App, 72–74

Job searches
LinkedIn and, 95–97
Profile and, 21

Lawyer Ratings app, 100
Lawyers
LinkedIn and, 1–2
LinkedIn user guide for, 5

Lawyer websites, advertising and, 88–89
Legal Updates app, 100
LinkedIn. *See also* Connections; Ethics; Participation; Profile(s)
  action steps for developing strategy for, 81–83
  confirming account for, 7–9
  creating account for, 7–10
  defined, 2
  general apps for, 99–101
  hiring process and, 95–97
  increasing visibility within, 20
  lawyers and, 1–2
  as marketing tool, 19
  resources for, 121–123
  sixty tips for, 115–120
  as social media, 1, 5
  Support page, 5
  "symmetrical" approach of, 26
LinkedIn Today, 69
Links
  Profile, 14–15

Marketing, LinkedIn and, 19
Misleading information, ethics and, 86
Mobile apps, monitoring via, 71–74
Model Rules, ABA. *See* ABA Model Rules
Monitoring
  about, 67–68
  benefits of network, 74
  via e-mail and RSS notifications, 70–71
  via Homepage method, 68–70
  via mobile apps, 71–74
MyTravel app, 100

Names, searching by, 43–45
Network monitoring, benefits of, 74

"100% complete" Profile, 17–18
Online reputation, managing, and Profile, 20–21

Participation. *See also* Connections; Profile(s)
  action steps, 82–83
  defined, 3
  effective use of, 51–52
  Groups, 54–58
  Updates, 52–54
"People You May Know" tool, 36–37, 70
Personal brand, managing, and Profile, 20–21
Photographs, profile, 13–14
Polls app, 100
Positions, listing, 16
Premium accounts, 9–10
Privacy-related settings, 77–78
"Products and Services" area, of Company Pages, 104
Professional headline, 15
Profile(s). *See also* Connections; Participation
  account, 78–79
  action steps, 81–82
  building initial, 11–12
  defined, 2
  editing, 12–16
  educational information in, 16
  improving search engine visibility of, 19–20
  job search and, 21
  linking, 14–15
  listing experience/positions information in, 16
  managing online reputation and, 20–21
  as marketing tool, 19
  methods for improving, 21–23
  "100% complete," 17–18
  photographs, 13–14

professional headline field in, 15
reasons for improving, 19–23
as resume, 21, 95–97
settings, 77
summary field in, 15–16
tips for making outstanding, 24
Projects and Teamspaces app, 100
Publications section, of Profile, 23

Questions
answering, 61
asking, 61

Reading List by Amazon app, 100
Recommendations
about, 62–63
for Company Pages, 104–105
for others, 63
receiving, 64
request tips, 65
Recommendations, ethics and, 91–92
Reputation, managing online, and
Profile, 20–21
Resources, for LinkedIn, 121–123
Resumes, using Profile for, 21,
95–97. *See also* Hiring process,
LinkedIn and
Rofo Real Estate Pro app, 100
RSS notifications
monitoring via, 70–71
Rules. *See* ABA Model Rules

Search engines, improving visibility
on, 19–20
Searching/searches
advanced techniques for, 107–113
alternate methods of, 46–49
companies, 109–111
existing connections for new
contacts, 45
groups, 112–113
by name, 43–45
taking advantage of power of
LinkedIn, 49–50

Settings
account, 78–79
Applications, 80
Companies, 80
e-mail, 79
Groups, 80
importance of, 75
privacy-related, 77–78
Profile, 77
starting, 76
Skills section, of Profile, 23
SlideShare Presentations app, 100
Social media, LinkedIn and, 1, 5
Solicitation, ethics and, 89–90
Sorting, search results, 108–109
Specialization, ethics and, 90
Specialties section, 15–16
Summary field, 15
Symmetrical approach, 26

Tips
Answer, 62
Company Pages, 105
for ethics, 92–93
for Groups, 56
for making Profile, 24
for Recommendations, 65
sixty, for LinkedIn, 115–120
Touches, 51–52
Tweets app, 100

Unauthorized practice of law, ethics
and, 91
Updates
defined, 52
items to include in, 52–53
reasons for posting, 53–54

Websites, lawyer, advertising and,
88–89
WordPress app, 100

SELECTED BOOKS FROM

The Lawyer's Guide to Collaboration Tools and Technologies: Smart Ways to Work Together
By Dennis Kennedy and Tom Mighell

Product Code: 5110589 / LPM Price: $59.95 / Regular Price: $89.95

This first-of-its-kind guide for the legal profession shows you how to use standard technology you already have and the latest "Web 2.0" resources and other tech tools, like Google Docs, Microsoft Office and Share-Point, and Adobe Acrobat, to work more effectively on projects with colleagues, clients, co-counsel and even opposing counsel. In *The Lawyer's Guide to Collaboration Tools and Technologies: Smart Ways to Work Together*, well-known legal technology authorities Dennis Kennedy and Tom Mighell provides a wealth of information useful to lawyers who are just beginning to try these tools, as well as tips and techniques for those lawyers with intermediate and advanced collaboration experience.

Google for Lawyers: Essential Search Tips and Productivity Tools
By Carole A. Levitt and Mark E. Rosch

Product Code: 5110704 / LPM Price: $47.95 / Regular Price: $79.95

This book introduces novice Internet searchers to the diverse collection of information locatable through Google. The book discusses the importance of including effective Google searching as part of a lawyer's due diligence, and cites case law that mandates that lawyers should use Google and other resources available on the Internet, where applicable. For intermediate and advanced users, the book unlocks the power of various advanced search strategies and hidden search features they might not be aware of.

The Lawyer's Guide to Adobe Acrobat, Third Edition
By David L. Masters

Product Code: 5110588 / LPM Price: $49.95 / Regular Price: $79.95

This book was written to help lawyers increase productivity, decrease costs, and improve client services by moving from paper-based files to digital records. This updated and revised edition focuses on the ways lawyers can benefit from using the most current software, Adobe® Acrobat 8, to create Portable Document Format (PDF) files.

PDF files are reliable, easy-to-use, electronic files for sharing, reviewing, filing, and archiving documents across diverse applications, business processes, and platforms. The format is so reliable that the federal courts' Case Management/Electronic Case Files (CM/ECF) program and state courts that use Lexis-Nexis File & Serve have settled on PDF as the standard.

You'll learn how to:

- Create PDF files from a number of programs, including Microsoft Office
- Use PDF files the smart way
- Markup text and add comments
- Digitally, and securely, sign documents
- Extract content from PDF files
- Create electronic briefs and forms

The Electronic Evidence and Discovery Handbook: Forms, Checklists, and Guidelines
By Sharon D. Nelson, Bruce A. Olson, and John W. Simek

Product Code: 5110569 / LPM Price: $99.95 / Regular Price: $129.95

The use of electronic evidence has increased dramatically over the past few years, but many lawyers still struggle with the complexities of electronic discovery. This substantial book provides lawyers with the templates they need to frame their discovery requests and provides helpful advice on what they can subpoena. In addition to the ready-made forms, the authors also supply explanations to bring you up to speed on the electronic discovery field. The accompanying CD-ROM features over 70 forms, including, Motions for Protective Orders, Preservation and Spoliation Documents, Motions to Compel, Electronic Evidence Protocol Agreements, Requests for Production, Internet Services Agreements, and more. Also included is a full electronic evidence case digest with over 300 cases detailed!

The Lawyer's Guide to Microsoft Word 2010
By Ben M. Schorr

Product Code: 5110721 / LPM Price: $41.95 / Regular Price: $69.95

Microsoft® Word is one of the most used applications in the Microsoft® Office suite. This handy reference includes clear explanations, legal-specific descriptions, and time-saving tips for getting the most out of Microsoft Word®—and customizing it for the needs of today's legal professional. Focusing on the tools and features that are essential for lawyers in their everyday practice, this book explains in detail the key components to help make you more effective, more efficient, and more successful.

The Lawyer's Guide to LexisNexis CaseMap
By Daniel J. Siegel

Product Code: 5110715 / LPM Price: $47.95 / Regular Price: $79.95

LexisNexis CaseMap is a computer program that makes analyzing cases easier and allows lawyers to do a better job for their clients in less time. Many consider this an essential law office tool. If you are interested in learning more about LexisNexis CaseMap, this book will help you:

- Analyze the strengths and weaknesses of your cases quickly and easily;
- Learn how to create files for people, organizations and issues, while avoiding duplication;
- Customize CaseMap so that you can get the most out of your data;
- Enter data so that you can easily prepare for trial, hearings, depositions, and motions for summary judgment;
- Import data from a wide range of programs, including Microsoft Outlook;
- Understand CaseMap's many Reports and ReportBooks;
- Use the Adobe DocPreviewer to import PDFs and quickly create facts and objects; and
- Learn how to perform advanced searches plus how to save and update your results.

SELECTED BOOKS FROM

Virtual Law Practice:
How to Deliver Legal Services Online
By Stephanie L. Kimbro

Product Code: 5110707 / LPM Price: $47.95 / Regular Price: $79.95

The legal market has recently experienced a dramatic shift as lawyers seek out alternative methods of practicing law and providing more affordable legal services. Virtual law practice is revolutionizing the way the public receives legal services and how legal professionals work with clients. If you are interested in this form of practicing law, *Virtual Law Practice* will help you:

- *Responsibly deliver legal services online to* your clients
- Successfully set up and operate a virtual law office
- Establish a virtual law practice online through a secure, client-specific portal
- Manage and market your virtual law practice
- Understand state ethics and advisory opinions
- Find more flexibility and work/life balance in the legal profession

The Lawyer's Essential Guide to Writing
By Marie Buckley

Product Code: 5110726 / LPM Price: $47.95 / Regular Price: $79.95

This is a readable, concrete guide to contemporary legal writing. Based on Marie Buckley's years of experience coaching lawyers, this book provides a systematic approach to all forms of written communication, from memoranda and briefs to e-mail and blogs. The book sets forth three principles for powerful writing and shows how to apply those principles to develop a clean and confident style.

iPad in One Hour for Lawyers
By Tom Mighell

Product Code: 5110719 / LPM Price: $19.95 / Regular Price: $34.95

Whether you are a new or a more advanced iPad user, *iPad in One Hour for Lawyers* takes a great deal of the mystery and confusion out of using your iPad. Ideal for lawyers who want to get up to speed swiftly, this book presents the essentials so you don't get bogged down in technical jargon and extraneous features and apps. In just six, short lessons, you'll learn how to:

- Quickly Navigate and Use the iPad User Interface
- Set Up Mail, Calendar, and Contacts
- Create and Use Folders to Multitask and Manage Apps
- Add Files to Your iPad, and Sync Them
- View and Manage Pleadings, Case Law, Contracts, and other Legal Documents
- Use Your iPad to Take Notes and Create Documents
- Use Legal-Specific Apps at Trial or in Doing Research

Find Info Like a Pro, Volume 1: Mining the Internet's Publicly Available Resources for Investigative Research
By Carole A. Levitt and Mark E. Rosch

Product Code: 5110708 / LPM Price: $47.95 / Regular Price: $79.95

This complete hands-on guide shares the secrets, shortcuts, and realities of conducting investigative and background research using the sources of publicly available information available on the Internet. Written for legal professionals, this comprehensive desk book lists, categorizes, and describes hundreds of free and fee-based Internet sites. The resources and techniques in this book are useful for investigations; depositions; locating missing witnesses, clients, or heirs; and trial preparation, among other research challenges facing legal professionals. In addition, a CD-ROM is included, which features clickable links to all of the sites contained in the book.

How to Start and Build a Law Practice, Platinum Fifth Edition
By Jay G Foonberg

Product Code: 5110508 / LPM Price: $57.95 / Regular Price: $69.95

This classic ABA bestseller has been used by tens of thousands of lawyers as the comprehensive guide to planning, launching, and growing a successful practice. It's packed with over 600 pages of guidance on identifying the right location, finding clients, setting fees, managing your office, maintaining an ethical and responsible practice, maximizing available resources, upholding your standards, and much more. You'll find the information you need to successfully launch your practice, run it at maximum efficiency, and avoid potential pitfalls along the way. If you're committed to starting—and growing—your own practice, this one book will give you the expert advice you need to make it succeed for years to come.

Social Media for Lawyers: The Next Frontier
By Carolyn Elefant and Nicole Black

Product Code: 5110710 / LPM Price: $47.95 / Regular Price: $79.95

The world of legal marketing has changed with the rise of social media sites such as Linkedin, Twitter, and Facebook. Law firms are seeking their companies attention with tweets, videos, blog posts, pictures, and online content. Social media is fast and delivers news at record pace. This book provides you with a practical, goal-centric approach to using social media in your law practice that will enable you to identify social media platforms and tools that fit your practice and implement them easily, efficiently, and ethically.

30-DAY RISK-FREE ORDER FORM

ABA **LawPracticeManagementSection**
MARKETING • MANAGEMENT • TECHNOLOGY • FINANCE

Please print or type. To ship UPS, we must have your street address.
If you list a P.O. Box, we will ship by U.S. Mail.

Name

Member ID

Firm/Organization

Street Address

City/State/Zip

Area Code/Phone (In case we have a question about your order)

E-mail

Method of Payment:
❑ Check enclosed, payable to American Bar Association
❑ MasterCard ❑ Visa ❑ American Express

Card Number   Expiration Date

Signature Required

MAIL THIS FORM TO:
American Bar Association, Publication Orders
P.O. Box 10892, Chicago, IL 60610

ORDER BY PHONE:
24 hours a day, 7 days a week:
Call 1-800-285-2221 to place a credit card order.
We accept Visa, MasterCard, and American Express.

EMAIL ORDERS: orders@americanbar.org
FAX: 1-312-988-5568

VISIT OUR WEB SITE: www.ShopABA.org
Allow 7-10 days for regular UPS delivery. Need it
sooner? Ask about our overnight delivery options.
Call the ABA Service Center at 1-800-285-2221
for more information.

GUARANTEE:
If—for any reason—you are not satisfied with your
purchase, you may return it within 30 days of receipt for
a refund of the price of the book(s). No questions asked.

Thank You For Your Order.

Join the ABA Law Practice Management Section today and receive a substantial discount on Section publications!

Product Code:	Description:	Quantity:	Price:	Total Price:
				$
				$
				$
				$
				$

**Shipping/Handling:		***Tax:**	Subtotal:	$
$0.00 to $9.99	add $0.00	IL residents add 9.5%	***Tax:**	$
$10.00 to $49.99	add $5.95	DC residents add 6%		
$50.00 to $99.99	add $7.95		****Shipping/Handling:**	$
$100.00 to $199.99	add $9.95	Yes, I am an ABA member and would like to join the Law Practice Management Section today! (Add $50.00)		$
$200.00 to $499.99	add $12.95		Total:	$